The Use of Data in Discrimination Issues Cases

William Rosenthal, Bernard Yancey, *Editors*

NEW DIRECTIONS FOR INSTITUTIONAL RESEARCH
PATRICK TERENZINI, *Editor-in-Chief*
MARVIN W. PETERSON, *Associate Editor*

Number 48, December 1985

Paperback sourcebooks in
The Jossey-Bass Higher Education Series

Jossey-Bass Inc., Publishers
San Francisco • London

William Rosenthal, Bernard Yancey (Eds.).
The Use of Data in Discrimination Issues Cases.
New Directions for Institutional Research, no. 48.
Volume XII, Number 4
San Francisco: Jossey-Bass, 1985

New Directions for Institutional Research
Patrick T. Terenzini, *Editor-in-Chief*
Marvin W. Peterson, *Associate Editor*

Copyright © 1985 by Jossey-Bass Inc., Publishers
                    and
                Jossey-Bass Limited

Copyright under International, Pan American, and Universal
Copyright Conventions. All rights reserved. No part of
this issue may be reproduced in any form—except for brief
quotation (not to exceed 500 words) in a review or professional
work—without permission in writing from the publishers.

New Directions for Institutional Research (publication number
USPS 098-830) is published quarterly by Jossey-Bass Inc., Publishers,
and is sponsored by the Association for Institutional Research.
The volume and issue numbers above are included for the
convenience of libraries. Second-class postage rates paid at
San Francisco, California, and at additional mailing offices.

Correspondence:
Subscriptions, single-issue orders, change of address notices,
undelivered copies, and other correspondence should be sent
to Subscriptions, Jossey-Bass Inc., Publishers, 433 California Street,
San Francisco, California 94104.

Editorial correspondence should be sent to the Editor-in-Chief,
Patrick T. Terenzini, Office of Institutional Research, SUNY,
Albany, New York 12222.

Library of Congress Catalog Card Number 85-60833

International Standard Serial Number ISSN 0271-0579

International Standard Book Number ISBN 87589-754-1

Cover art by WILLI BAUM

Manufactured in the United States of America

Ordering Information

The paperback sourcebooks listed below are published quarterly and can be ordered either by subscription or single-copy.

Subscriptions cost $40.00 per year for institutions, agencies, and libraries. Individuals can subscribe at the special rate of $30.00 per year *if payment is by personal check*. (Note that the full rate of $40.00 applies if payment is by institutional check, even if the subscription is designated for an individual.) Standing orders are accepted.

Single copies are available at $9.95 when payment accompanies order, and *all single-copy orders under $25.00 must include payment*. (California, New Jersey, New York, and Washington, D.C., residents please include appropriate sales tax.) For billed orders, cost per copy is $9.95 plus postage and handling. (Prices subject to change without notice.)

Bulk orders (ten or more copies) of any individual sourcebook are available at the following discounted prices: 10-49 copies, $8.95 each; 50-100 copies, $7.96 each; over 100 copies, *inquire*. Sales tax and postage and handling charges apply as for single copy orders.

To ensure correct and prompt delivery, all orders must give either the *name of an individual* or an *official purchase order number*. Please submit your order as follows:

Subscriptions: specify series and year subscription is to begin.
Single Copies: specify sourcebook code (such as, IR1) and first two words of title.

Mail orders for United States and Possessions, Latin America, Canada, Japan, Australia, and New Zealand to:
Jossey-Bass Inc., Publishers
433 California Street
San Francisco, California 94104

Mail orders for all other parts of the world to:
Jossey-Bass Limited
28 Banner Street
London EC1Y 8QE

New Directions for Institutional Research Series
Patrick T. Terenzini, *Editor-in-Chief*
Marvin W. Peterson, *Associate Editor*

IR1 *Evaluating Institutions for Accountability*, Howard R. Bowen
IR2 *Assessing Faculty Effort*, James I. Doi
IR3 *Toward Affirmative Action*, Lucy W. Sells
IR4 *Organizing Nontraditional Study*, Samuel Baskin
IR5 *Evaluating Statewide Boards*, Robert O. Berdahl
IR6 *Assuring Academic Progress Without Growth*, Allan M. Cartter

IR7   *Responding to Changing Human Resource Needs,* Raul Heist,
      Jonathan R. Warren
IR8   *Measuring and Increasing Academic Productivity,* Robert A. Wallhaus
IR9   *Assessing Computer-Based System Models,* Thomas R. Mason
IR10 *Examining Departmental Management,* James Smart, James Montgomery
IR11 *Allocating Resources Among Departments,* Paul L. Dressel,
      Lou Anna Kimsey Simon
IR12 *Benefiting from Interinstitutional Research,* Marvin W. Peterson
IR13 *Applying Analytic Methods to Planning and Management,*
      David S. P. Hopkins, Roger G. Scroeder
IR14 *Protecting Individual Rights to Privacy in Higher Education,*
      Alton L. Taylor
IR15 *Appraising Information Needs of Decision Makers,* Carl R. Adams
IR16 *Increasing the Public Accountability of Higher Education,* John K. Folger
IR17 *Analyzing and Constructing Cost,* Meredith A. Gonyea
IR18 *Employing Part-Time Faculty,* David W. Leslie
IR19 *Using Goals in Research and Planning,* Robert Fenske
IR20 *Evaluating Faculty Performance and Vitality,* Wayne C. Kirschling
IR21 *Developing a Total Marketing Plan,* John A. Lucas
IR22 *Examining New Trends in Administrative Computing,* E. Michael Staman
IR23 *Professional Development for Institutional Research,* Robert G. Cope
IR24 *Planning Rational Retrenchment,* Alfred L. Cooke
IR25 *The Impact of Student Financial Aid on Institutions,* Joe B. Henry
IR26 *The Autonomy of Public Colleges,* Paul L. Dressel
IR27 *Academic Program Evaluation,* Eugene C. Craven
IR28 *Academic Planning for the 1980s,* Richard B. Heydinger
IR29 *Institutional Assessment for Self-Improvement,* Richard I. Miller
IR30 *Coping with Faculty Reduction,* Stephen R. Hample
IR31 *Evaluation of Management and Planning Systems,* Nick L. Poulton
IR32 *Increasing the Use of Program Evaluation,* Jack Lindquist
IR33 *Effective Planned Change Strategies,* G. Melvin Hipps
IR34 *Qualitative Methods for Institutional Research,* Eileen Kuhns,
      S. V. Martorana
IR35 *Information Technology: Advances and Applications,* Bernard Sheehan
IR36 *Studying Student Attrition,* Ernest T. Pascarella
IR37 *Using Research for Strategic Planning,* Norman P. Uhl
IR38 *The Politics and Pragmatics of Institutional Research,* James W. Firnberg,
      William F. Lasher
IR39 *Applying Methods and Techniques of Futures Research,* James L. Morrison,
      William L. Renfro, Wayne I. Boucher
IR40 *College Faculty: Versatile Human Resources in a Period of Constraint,*
      Roger G. Baldwin, Robert T. Blackburn
IR41 *Determining the Effectiveness of Campus Services,* Robert A. Scott
IR42 *Issues in Pricing Undergraduate Education,* Larry H. Litten
IR43 *Responding to New Realities in Funding,* Larry L. Leslie
IR44 *Using Microcomputers for Planning and Management Support,*
      William L. Tetlow
IR45 *Impact and Challenges of a Changing Federal Role,*
      Virginia Ann Hodgkinson
IR46 *Institutional Research in Transition,* Marvin W. Peterson, Mary Corcoran
IR47 *Assessing Educational Outcomes,* Peter T. Ewell

Contents

Editors' Notes 1
William Rosenthal, Bernard Yancey

Chapter 1. Social Issues and Social Remedies: 3
The Study of Racism and Sexism on Campus
James L. Litwin
An approach to the study of racism and sexism on campus, including the politics and research methods required.

Chapter 2. Preparation, Prevention, and Response: 19
Data Elements and Data Bases for Support
Celia Allard, Ira W. Langston, Frank A. Schmidtlein
Issues related to data collection, storage, maintenance, and usage as governed by the institution's situation.

Chapter 3. Responding to Litigation: 35
The Roles and Strategies of Researchers in Court Cases
Bernard Yancey
An overview of social issues legislation, the litigation process, and the roles of the members of the institution's "team," as well as a discussion of strategies appropriate at various points in the process.

Chapter 4. Statistical Issues and Concerns in Court Cases 65
Dennis D. Hengstler, Gerald W. McLaughlin
A review and critique of statistical methods common to social issues litigation and a discussion of methods that may be more precise, useful tools than classic regression approaches.

Chapter 5. Changing Conditions, Changing Responses: 83
A Case Study of Minority Participation in Indiana Higher Education
John A. Muffo
A statewide attempt to understand the causes of minority underrepresentation in higher education and to address those causes rather than accept the relatively modest changes resulting from court-mandated hiring guidelines.

Concluding Remarks 97
William Rosenthal, Bernard Yancey

Index 103

The Association for Institutional Research was created in 1966 to benefit, assist, and advance research leading to improved understanding, planning, and operation of institutions of higher education. Publication policy is set by its Publications Board.

PUBLICATIONS BOARD
Stephen R. Hample (Chairperson), Montana State University
Ellen E. Chaffee, National Center for Higher Education Management Systems
Jean J. Endo, University of Colorado at Boulder
Cameron L. Fincher, University of Georgia
Richard B. Heydinger, University of Minnesota
Penny A. Wallhaus, Illinois Community College Board

EX-OFFICIO MEMBERS OF THE PUBLICATIONS BOARD
Charles F. Elton, University of Kentucky
Elizabeth F. Fox, University of Alabama in Birmingham
Gerald W. McLaughlin, Virginia Polytechnic Institute & State University
Marvin W. Peterson, University of Michigan
Patrick T. Terenzini, State University of New York at Albany

EDITORIAL ADVISORY BOARD
All members of the Publications Board and:
Frederick E. Balderston, University of California, Berkeley
Howard R. Bowen, Claremont Graduate School
Roberta D. Brown, Arkansas College
Lyman A. Glenny, University of California, Berkeley (retired)
David S. P. Hopkins, Stanford University
Roger G. Schroeder, University of Minnesota
Robert J. Silverman, Ohio State University
Martin A. Trow, University of California, Berkeley

For information about the Association for Institutional Research, write:

    AIR Executive Office
    314 Stone Building
    Florida State University
    Tallahassee, FL 32306

    (904) 644-4470

Editors' Notes

The following chapters have developed from discussion of equity and discrimination over the past several years among members of the researchers and the Courts' Special Interest Group of The Association for Institutional Research. They represent first, an attempt to examine forces that have resulted in social action litigation against institutions of higher education; second, an attempt to present an overview of legal, data base, and statistical issues that are likely to effect the work of the research office that supports its institution before, during, or after litigation; and third, an attempt to indicate directions institutions and their researchers may wish to consider in the next period of response to current social issues. Although much of this volume is about the procedures for handling data relative to litigation or the possibility of litigation, we have chosen to open and close the volume with chapters that discuss methods of dealing with social and equity issues outside the context of litigation. This format indicates our belief that the real responsibility for equal opportunity in higher education belongs not to courts or legislatures, but to the institutions of higher education themselves.

In his chapter on social issues and social remedies, Litwin traces the background of social discrimination issues on campus and develops a plan for their study outside the framework of the court case. This chapter might well be read as a treatise on developing programs to avoid litigation, although its intentions are broader. Allard, Langston, and Schmidtlein's chapter on preparation, prevention, and response discusses questions relating to litigation from the view of developing a data base and a data base philosophy before litigation occurs as well as after the institution becomes involved in litigation. This chapter, like Litwin's, may be read with a view toward correcting problems rather than preparing for the inevitable consequences of their neglect.

Yancey's chapter on responding to litigation is both guide for the research office that provides support to legal staff and a guide for an administration in how to conduct the institution's response to a suit. It traces legal issues and the responses both sides are likely to make to those issues, and it suggests approaches to making the institution's responses as effective as possible. In Chapter Four, Hengstler and McLaughlin discuss statistical techniques that have figured in equity studies as well as equity suits, and they introduce discussions of methods that deserve consideration as alternatives to those currently favored by the courts.

In a time when courts are playing a lesser role in civil rights reform in higher education, Muffo's chapter on changing responses follows one state coordinating board's attempt to go beyond current court-ordered or court-inspired responses to the small number of minority members in higher education by investigating and treating the causes of the problem. We believe that Muffo's analysis of the problem and plan for change suggest an important direction in responding to the social issues that have figured heavily in the court cases of recent years. We find this study an excellent example of the practical application of those principles Litwin discusses in Chapter One; a response to the social issues themselves rather than to court-imposed guidelines.

This is not to suggest that the period of litigation and response to litigation is over (the occurrence of age discrimination cases in the recent past certainly suggests otherwise) but that institutions of higher education have the opportunity to use their considerable resources to seek remedies for the inequities that result in litigation rather than merely as tools for coping with the courts.

William Rosenthal
Bernard Yancey
Editors

William Rosenthal is professor of institutional and analytic studies in the Office of Planning and Budgets at Michigan State University. He is currently involved in the development of large, mainframe-based analytic systems and in micro-to-mainframe applications.

Bernard Yancey, a research associate in the Office of the Dean of Students at the University of Texas at Austin, has been an expert witness in a variety of labor litigation cases and has conducted numerous workshops concerning the use of computers and statistics.

Personal and institutional racism and sexism have not been eradicated, and the policies implemented a few years ago have not necessarily changed practices and behaviors, even though they may have driven some underground.

Social Issues and Social Remedies: The Study of Racism and Sexism on Campus

James L. Litwin

Taking Sides

The establishment of equity between sexes and races on campus is a major social, political, economic, and legal issue. Various strategies and practices are being debated as institutions struggle to minimize the damage and maximize returns. However, there are racial and sexual issues in addition to equity that also demand institutional attention.

In the 1960s, colleges and universities that had been predominantly white opened their doors to minorities, and in the 1970s women began to redefine their institutional roles and situations. Institutional responses included visible offices for minority affairs,

The author wishes to acknowledge the support and critiques of three colleagues: Dr. Stuart Terrass of the University of Akron and Dr. Winifred Stone and Ms. Suzanne Crawford of Bowling Green State University.

women's studies centers, ethnic studies departments, feminist scholarship, and ombudspersons. These reforms were thought to have stabilized relationships and eased strife. After all, not only had access been provided but official guardians had been appointed.

However, racial and sexual stereotyping and harassment persist on today's campus. Personal and institutional racism and sexism have not been eradicated, and the policies implemented a few years ago have not significantly changed practices and behaviors, even though they may have driven some underground. According to one steering committee on the status of women and minorities: "The strides that we have made also disguise many of the problems. The problems have become hidden, less obvious, and some have been dealt with, but the great remainder are basic. The second generation of reforms and changes must be made. They must be just as dramatic and visible as the first, perhaps even more so because they must be sweeping in nature and institutional in scope" (Crawford and others, 1982, p. 1).

Colleges and universities are not always eager to examine these experiences. Public research on racism and sexism seems to have been done mostly by academic and not by institutional researchers. The following are some reasons for this apparent paucity of institutional studies:

1. Institutional studies on discrimination are done in-house and their subsequent circulation may be restricted. This is understandable; discrimination of any sort is nasty business, and identifiable discrimination can be embarrassing, if not damning. There is no legal obligation to share these data. On the other hand, noncirculation limits the awareness of other researchers and deprives them of possible support needed for initiating studies on their own campus.

2. Institutional researchers have a number of important issues to deal with, including budgets, enrollment, planning, and so on. Studies of minorities and women are extremely complex and often do not become a priority until there is a public crisis. (Also, institutional researchers do not usually determine institutional priorities. However, there are often more opportunities for input to the institutional agenda than many practitioners admit.)

3. Institutional researchers share the myth that sexism and racism do not exist on campus, or that these phenomena are not subject to improvement, that is, that sexism and racism are deeply ingrained attitudes and reflect the general problem of society.

4. Most institutional researchers do not belong to minority

groups, and only recently have women entered the profession in significant numbers. Thus, most institutional researchers have not experienced racial or sexual injustices personally, and they may either not recognize their seriousness or find themselves reluctant to speak for others.

5. Minorities' and women's issues are tied to the politics and the sociology of the institution. Studies of racism are closely watched. Sanctions may be involved. Value judgments come into play. By training, most institutional researchers proceed with caution when they approach sensitive areas that call for moral and ethical judgments. Ambiguous results can easily lead to no-win situations for institutional research offices. Farrell (1984) points up the wide diversity of opinion on the role of institutional research and involvement in decision making.

6. There is no consensus on these issues. Views on racism and sexism may not be shared by colleagues on campus, especially by administrators who fear not being able to manage the consequences and conclusions of studies of racism and sexism.

These reasons for inaction are not insurmountable, neither is the list meant to be antagonistic. Obviously, institutional issues such as student outcomes and faculty productivity must be addressed, and many routine studies must be maintained. There are four important arguments, though, in favor of initiating studies of racism and sexism. First, racism and sexism have not disappeared. The fact that there are some advocates and guardians only protects minorities and women from some of the worst and most overt abuses. A wide range of studies is available: Allen and others (1982), Anderson and others (1984), Astin (1982), Berg and Ferber (1983), Cones and others (1983), Dziech and Weiner (1984), Engelmayer (1983), Maihoff and Forrest (1983), Project on the Status and Education of Women (1984b), Smith (1980), and Thomas (1981). Each of these studies has limitations, and some points are arguable, but when considered as a composite, they are persuasive. Faculty, staff, and students may desire to be understanding and enlightened; however, the research suggests that either knowingly or unknowingly they are behaving in racist and sexist ways.

Second, issues of racism and sexism are not minority or women's problems alone. They demand institutional ownership. The negative consequences of any acts of discrimination rebound and diminish all faculty, staff, and students.

Third, racism and sexism are generally not the effects of something else gone wrong. They are major contributing causes to an environment in which separation and indifference exist for minority students and in which women struggle against societal and occupational stereotypes.

Fourth, institutional research offices can bring credibility to the study of racism and sexism, since they are not associated with vested interest groups. Centers for women, student affairs offices, minority affairs offices, and developmental education departments often carry out reliable and valid studies that are discounted because they are seen as self-serving. Results are "accepted," but desired changes are not made.

While it is possible that critics will accuse the institutional researcher of being one-sided, this charge can be countered with openness and candor. In any case, it is a risk worth taking. Dziech and Weiner (1984, p. 1) argue that "our experiences revealed that the silence is part of the problem, that ignoring the issue only makes it worse."

Steps in Design

Once the administration and the institutional research office have decided to initiate and support studies of racism or sexism, there are still practical and methodological hurdles to overcome. These include:

Keeping Institutional Statistics. Data by gender are usually accurate and easy to keep. However, racial data are frequently inaccurate. Quite often these data depend on the students' consent to identify themselves. There are several reasons students may choose not to cooperate. Students may feel that racial identification will lead to separate treatment and being singled out for their reactions to and participation in special programs. Racial identification can lead to harmful presuppositions about ability and interest. When students are not identified by race, however, random sampling to ensure sufficient numbers of minority student respondents can become time-consuming and costly.

Student headcounts are the most natural and unobtrusive method of collecting data. Other institutional data on students can, of course, be kept—for example, academic performance and withdrawals. Academic performance is obviously necessary. If students do not perform at an acceptable level, they may be expelled. It is also necessary to study these data for extended periods of time. Because minority students are sometimes disproportionally enrolled in special entry programs, they are usually tracked for a short period of time. Minority student performance in programs after their initial entrance is often not followed. Institutional responsibility, though, does not end after students enter college. Minority students must be persisters and graduates in order to diversify the accountability of the institution. Panos (1981) has shown the importance of using retention and alumni data to develop an empirical base for determining program success.

Keeping academic measures and demographic data however is the lesser of the statistics problems—it is often bureaucratic and technical, more an information problem of the sort to which institutional researchers are accustomed. Gathering social data and social measures is more problematic.

Agreeing on Terms. There are few, if any, indicators of racism and sexism that are agreed on. Legal definitions do not always serve us well, even though they are useful in equity cases. (Most instances of bias and discrimination in this context are not illegal but are nevertheless destructive of human relations.)

Metha and Nigg (1983) suggest that a specific, formal definition of sexual harassment rather than a self-definition, as well as persistent follow up resulted in a lower proportion of recurrent incidents in their research. They found that 13 percent of the students in their most recent study reported incidents of sexual harassment whereas several earlier studies had reported incidents at rates of 25 to 40 percent.

Definitions can be highly formal or highly personalized. In either case they will have an impact on response patterns. Blanshan (1983, p. 16) offered this definition: "Sexual harassment is the unwanted imposition of sexual requirements in the context of a relationship of unequal power." In the same review (p. 17), another experientially based definition is used to define sexual harrassment: "When women are made to feel uncomfortable in classes where sexist jokes are continually told, when women feel that they risk a proposition or assault if they socialize with academic associates, when women are thought odd and so labeled for pursuing a male-dominated program, when women must avoid mentoring relationships to avoid pressure for sexual relationships, they are experiencing sexual harassment." The impact of these definitions on a respondent wondering if she has experienced sexual harassment is obvious.

In an article commenting on definitions of sexual harassment, Crocker (1983, p. 697) suggests that "no definition will satisfy everyone in the university community: many will be threatened and defensive; others will find it unnecessary, restrictive, silly, even morally offensive; but still others will welcome recognition of an ugly and pervasive problem." To wrestle continually with definitional boundaries is a trap. To postpone study because there is no available consensual definition is to succumb to a specious argument.

Studies of racism and sexism often focus on social relations between races and sexes outside of the classroom. However, the social aspects of the classroom, especially the general distortions and myths that accompany minorities and women into the classroom, have been of recent interest. Women have recently addressed the use of language in the classroom and the variety of jokes and comments meant to flatter but which actually patronize or demean women. Hall and others (1982) provide examples of these interactions as do Dziech and Weiner (1984) and Cones and others (1983). Hall and others (1982, p. 3) point up: "Whether overt or subtle, differential treatment based on sex is far from innocuous; its cumulative effects can be damaging not only to individual women and men but also to the educational process itself." Katz (1983, p. 36) adds "Racism is so much a part of the texture of our culture that professors will often make stereotyped comments about blacks without being aware of the hurtful impact."

The area of sexism produces other quandaries. Besides discrimination and harassment, sexual assault can also be a problem. Sexual assault usually means rape, and rape is a violent, criminal act that cannot be qualified. Describing sexual assault as "date-rape" or "acquaintance" rape may illuminate some aspects of a rape situation for students, but it makes rape no less devastating. It may make the institution nervous to talk about rape publicly, but the need to educate young men and women is paramount.

The study of racism has a long history in society and on college campuses, but it is not free of definitional problems. Allen and others, (1982, p. 9) in a preliminary report to a national study, say that students report frequent exposure to racial discrimination, but an interesting qualification is noted: "In general, students reported fairly poor relationships with white faculty, staff, and students on their campus. These relationships were rated good to excellent when students evaluated them in terms of their personal interactions with white faculty, staff, and students." Thus, students' responses depended on whether they were being asked about general race relations or personal experiences. There is an arbitrariness to social data that can be dissatisfying, and the definitional issues are certainly not neat and clean. The debate is important, but the goal of reducing all aspects of racism and sexism should not be lost in the process.

Agreeing on the Problem. Solving the definitional issues partially resolves another related task. What is the nature of the problem and the general purpose to be served by the study of racism and sexism? There are several versions of this question that can prove troublesome. The first version comes in the form of "proving" that racism and sexism exist. If a particular attitude or behavior discriminates or harasses, does it prove that racism or sexism exists? Was the incident an accident, coincidence, or misinterpretation? There are many forms of denial, all of which chip away at the integrity of the victim. Jenkins (1983, p. 4) argues that "Professors may declare with either surprise or chagrin that they do not stereotype and are not sexist." Jenkins says that sex biases are so accepted within the culture that they have "remained almost invisible—or, when visible, have been viewed as innocuous." Menges and Exum (1983, p. 139) suggest that "evidence of overt discrimination is difficult to gather. What discrimination exists in postsecondary education is likely to be expressed subtly and indirectly."

Institutional studies must stay at the level of showing that patterns exist and that the frequency with which they happen is more than chance. Studies should not be forced to show that maliciousness exists (although it may). Examining behavior and consequences is difficult, attributing causation is problematic, but divining motivation is impossible and not necessary to the development of preventative programs.

There is a second version of agreeing on the problem that can also complicate matters: Should *personal* or *institutional* racism and sexism be sought out? The answer is clearly both, but agreeing on an approach is another question. Institutional racism is not the sum total of all the individual acts of racism and sexism. It refers to those practices, policies, and traditions that are imbedded in the institution and that can be attached to no particular person. It encompasses the lack of role models, the distribution of funding, special program arrangements, assumptions about career patterns, residential arrangements, student-athlete stereotypes, and the hiring of faculty and staff.

Personal racism and sexism, ironically, are easier to locate but harder to solve than institutional racism and sexism. The attitudes of students and professors can be identified but are difficult to change. Behaviors can be cited, but sanctions are difficult to apply. Academic freedom and free speech are called on to defend certain actions. Victims are said to not understand or to lack a sense of humor.

Other issues must be agreed on. Where racism or sexism is found, who will address it? What changes will be made? Will these studies be continued, or are they one-shot studies? Will various interpretations and feedback be gathered? Will the study become public? Metha and Nigg (1983, p. 15) point out that as a result of their work "One thing is certain: The issue of sexual harassment is no longer a 'closet concern' but rather a general concern of students, faculty, and staff that is being discussed in an open and honest manner. What began as a committee concern has become a major university commitment."

Selecting Methods. There is no standard set of tactics by which to reduce the risks of entering controversial territory. However, there is often a sterility to these data. They often need to be buttressed by observations of the constituency. One of the problems is that quantitative data has a certain appeal; "anecdotal" data are dismissed. Yet, personal stories are powerful and convincing. Data should not be quantified to the extent that they do not provide the impact necessary to promote change. Arpad (1984, p. 6) noted that after a number of quantitative studies had been done on the status of women and minorities at her institution: "These studies were usually read by a few administrators and then filed. We chose this format—particularly the telling of individual stories—because we hoped that they would be rhetorically effective in convincing a large and diverse audience that a problem existed; we hoped that if the audience could recognize the discomfort and pain of individuals in their community, they would feel an urgency about making changes to create a climate that would be supportive to all members of our heterogeneous population."

The pros and cons of some common social research methods need to be considered:

1. *Survey Questionnaires.* Most surveys are created by the institution because national companies have not developed comprehensive measures of campus sexism and racism. Reliability and validity are questionable in homemade instruments, but they do have the great advantage of dealing with the institution's specific programs. The group process of designing a survey questionnaire can also be valuable in preparing an institution for a particular study. A number of works identified in this chapter can be used as source material for questions. Bogart and others (1981) have provided a useful model for many.

2. *Student Ratings of Instruction.* Surely there will be arguments for and against using student ratings of instruction, but there are few areas more important to academe than faculty-student interactions. The "Student Perception Questionnaire" developed as part of an investigation of introductory courses in the social sciences is a useful model in this area (Jenkins, 1983).

3. *In-depth Interviews.* Interviews have a great advantage in that many incidents of racism and sexism have a uniquely personal side to them. Who and what offended a student are questions better handled in an interview than on a survey form. Answers however, must be presented in a coherent manner. Hall and others' (1982) "Chilly Climate" makes good use of interviews with faculty involved in teaching minority students.

4. *Group Interviews.* A variation of the individual interview is the group interview wherein investigators meet with a group of students, faculty, or staff. This technique has the advantage of discovering areas of agreement and amplifying the facets of an issue. The danger is that accusations can snowball, but open participation within the academic community can also be affirmed.

5. *Public Meetings.* Commissions and task forces can meet with specific target groups, but they can also announce public meetings and give interested groups the time to organize their views and arguments. This setting must ensure that all groups have a fair chance to be heard. Public meetings tend to be one-sided treatments of the issues, though, because groups or individuals are unlikely to come forward to deny or minimize racism and sexism.

6. *Qualitative Research.* Study modes such as naturalistic inquiry, anthropological research, and illuminative evaluation have the advantage of being less obtrusive, but they also consume energy and time. However, they are particularly appropriate if racism and sexism are seen as part of the larger culture. Patton (1982, p. 9) observes that "the holistic approach assumes that the whole is greater than the sum of its parts . . . it is insufficient simply to study and measure the parts of a situation by gathering data about isolated variables, scales, or dimensions."

7. *Single-Group versus Comparison Studies.* A criticism of these research initiatives is that sexism and racism will always be found if one wants to find them. Some of this criticism can be skirted by comparison studies wherein both men and women or majority and minority students are included. Questionnaires, therefore, do not ask students or faculty to make judgments about the ways they are treated based on race or sex. Instead, studies examine

differences between group responses. Traditional statistical tests using gender or race can then be used to examine the differences.

The comparison study has the drawback that, should both groups experience poor faculty-student interaction, for instance, there may be a tendency to deny the seriousness of the problem. Such problems need to be addressed even if they are not disproportionally suffered by minorities or women. (It is also possible to find that groups are treated in a similar fashion but for very different reasons.) Another important outcome of the comparison strategy is that some myths may be challenged. Gosman and others (1983) found that multiple regression analyses show that racial differences disappear when the effects of other students and institutional characteristics are controlled.

Starting Up

Due to the controversial nature of the study of racism and sexism, the institutional researcher must use careful planning and consideration. The institutional researcher must not only be the methodologist but must give equal attention to group process and institutional dynamics. Each college and university has its own idiosyncrasies and institutional memories that must be considered. Here are some general considerations to keep in mind:

Commitment of Top Administration to the Study. No college or university president enjoys being surprised by the announced results of studies, and certainly any social remedies pursued will need the full support and resources of major administrators.

Peterson and others (1979, p. 280) note that "the institutional responses to black students were related to an overall climate of concern with and commitment to dealing with racial issues." Hitt and others (1983, p. 400) found that "commitment from higher administration and a receptive attitude on the part of key university personnel" were the two most important criteria of affirmative action program effectiveness.

Dean Henry Rosovsky at Harvard (Project on the Status and Education of Women, 1984a, p. 2) sent to every faculty member and student in the Faculty of Arts and Sciences this closing comment to a letter on the topic of sexual harassment: "I have written this letter so that every member of the faculty might be aware of these discussions, and of my own views."

Advisory Panels. The input of major groups on campus—faculty senate, minority and majority students, and men and women—should be gathered. While a blue-ribbon commission or task force approach can also be used, it has the disadvantage of appearing more highly ideological than it is in reality and often generates the one-shot approach rather than systematic and continuing study.

Networking. If certain ideologies are put forward, they should not be discounted, but embraced for their insights. Do not duplicate what has already been done but build on knowledge wherever possible. Research done by women's groups and minority groups can be incorporated; an "us (neutral, objective observers) versus them (vested interest groups)" view of research will be unproductive. Institutional researchers need to communicate with others, not only to gain ideas and build resources, but also to have other offices endorse their work and anticipate its arrival.

Definitions. There are many functional definitions that can be used to develop a broad agreement on what is being studied. Those whose personal definitions are ignored will become nay sayers. Arriving at a definition is an important part of the group process.

Clear Purpose of Study. Is the intention of the study to establish that an undercurrent of complaint is based in overt and covert racist and sexist behavior? Or is the purpose to stimulate dialogue and heighten awareness of potential discrimination? Decide who the audience is—those working for change or those to be convinced. The argument and supporting data must be suited to the intended purposes and audiences.

Appropriate Strategies and Research Methods. A "60 Minutes" style research for wrongdoing may be forceful in the short term, but traditional survey research methods may have greater overall impact. Combinations of research methods should be considered. In addition, the researcher should decide whether to include both sexual and racial issues in the same study. Should there be a series of inquiries? These topics taken together may be too large to receive adequate treatment—both in terms of a single study and in terms of corrective actions.

Familiarity with the Major Works in the Area. Such familiarity will provide perspective and place the research in context. Institutional reports, opinion pieces, and journals, in addition to the works mentioned in this chapter, should be consulted, though some contextual factors may still not be discussed. The number of studies available is expanding—in 1983, Maihoff and Forrest reported they had found only two university surveys on sexual harassment. Due to groups like the Project on the Status and Education of Women and the Ford Foundation, more visibility has been given to the issues, and more study has been initiated. Some other works include Astin (1982) and a related critique by Fincher (1982); Astin and Kent (1983); Brown and others (1980); Duran (1983); Franklin and others (1981); Gartland and Bevilacqua (1983); Thomas (1981); and Verba and others (1983).

Criticism. The fact that a study is being conducted may generate an accusation of cover-up on the one side and witch-hunting on the other. A study may also be accused of being a token effort, a superficial way to deal with problems, or something that is being done to mollify certain irritating elements in the community. There will not be unanimity on the need to conduct these studies or on the value of the results.

Initial Disappointment. Racism and sexism are heated social and political issues. When the study findings are published, minorities may say "we already know that." Others will say that nothing can be done. Probably little will change immediately, but the situation may be prevented from getting worse. The data will probably support the development and adoption of racial and sexual harassment and discrimination policies if such policies do not already exist. Grievance procedures, training programs, workshops, and the placement of relevant items in self-studies and rating forms may also be incorporated. Future reform efforts will eventually draw on these data for support.

In Conclusion

It is tempting to use clichés, to take postures, or to act morally indignant when discussing racism and sexism. The opposite may also be attractive: to be cool, to be "rational," to be indifferent to the outcome. The institutional researcher who becomes involved in sexism or racism studies will need a bit of the activist-reformer orientation. Terrass and Pomrenke (1981, p. 15) suggest that "institutional researchers too often deal as if their world were only rational: They must learn to function well at social, emotional, and political levels."

No matter how the institutional researcher tried to limit such studies to descriptive purposes, the studies will be used ultimately for prescriptive purposes, and therefore, these purposes need to be considered in the shaping and design of studies. Every institutional study is launched because a need to know has been established.

Some studies are done so routinely that we have forgotten why they are done at all. The prescriptive element becomes heightened in studies of such controversial issues as racism and sexism. A conclusion drawn by Menges and Exum (1983, p. 139) is both a slap on the wrist and an encouragement: "In our view, slow progress is less the result of deliberately prejudiced actions than the failure of persons of good will to ensure equity."

The study of racism and sexism needs institutional research involvement. Though fraught with ambiguity, it should not be put off because of uncertainty or because it deals with value issues. McPherson (1983, p. 273) argues that "a vital question is whether the higher education community will be able to summon the energy and resources to address them [value issues] in a reflective and constructive way. There is little reason to expect that 'benign neglect' or laissez faire will produce a desirable outcome."

Institutional researchers need to say they will not tolerate racism and sexism. Dziech and Weiner (1984, p. 186) argue that "the very act of analyzing the problem should lead naturally to an intellectual and psychological breakthrough for institutions, administrators, faculty, and students." The issues are complex, ambiguous, and difficult, just the kind of problems that institutional researchers have the expertise and credibility to handle.

References

Allen, W. R., Daughtry, D., and Wilson, K. *Preliminary Report: Winter 1981 Study of Black Undergraduate Students Attending Predominantly White, State-Supported Universities.* Ann Arbor: Center for Afro-American and African Studies, The University of Michigan, 1982.

Anderson, R., and others. *President's Task Force on Minority Student Needs.* Bowling Green, Ohio: Bowling Green State University, 1984.

Arpad, S. Personal communication accompanying S. Crawford and others. Bowling Green, Ohio: Bowling Green State University, 1984.

Astin, A. *Minorities in American Higher Education.* San Francisco: Jossey-Bass, 1982.

Astin, H., and Kent, L. "Gender Roles in Transition: Research and Policy Implementation for Higher Education." *Journal of Higher Education,* 1983, 54 (3), 309-324.

Bender, E., Burk, B., and Walker, N. (Eds.). *All of Us Are Present* (Stephens College Symposium). Columbia, Mo.: James Madison Wood Research Institute, 1984.

Berg, H., and Ferber, M. "Men and Women Graduate Students: Who Succeeds and Why?" *Journal of Higher Education,* 1983, 54 (6), 629-648.

Blanshan, S. A. "Activism, Research, and Policy: Sexual Harassment." *Journal of the National Association for Women Deans, Administrators, and Counselors,* 1983, 46 (2), 16-22.

Bogart, K., Flagle, J., and Jung, S. *Institutional Self-Study Guide on Sex Equity.*

Washington, D.C.: American Institutes for Research, 1981.
Brown, G., and others. *The Condition of Education for Hispanic Americans.* Washington, D.C.: National Center for Education Statistics, 1980.
Cones, J.H., III, Noonan, J. F., and Janha, D. (Eds.). *Teaching Minority Students.* New Directions for Teaching and Learning, no. 16. San Francisco: Jossey-Bass, 1983.
Crawford, S., and others. *Report on the Status of Women and Minorities.* Bowling Green, Ohio: Bowling Green State University, 1982.
Crocker, P. "An Analysis of University Definitions of Sexual Harassment." *Signs: Journal of Women in Culture and Society,* 1983, *8* (4), 696-707.
Duran, R. *Hispanics' Education and Background: Predictors of College Achievement.* New York: College Entrance Examination Board, 1983.
Dziech, B. W., and Weiner, L. *The Lecherous Professor: Sexual Harassment on Campus.* Boston: Beacon Press, 1984.
Englemayer, P. "Campus Crime." *Wall Street Journal, LXIV* (27), November 21, 1983, pp. 1 and 18.
Farrell, J. "Institutional Research and Decision Making: A Bibliographic Essay." *Research in Higher Education,* 1984, *20* (3), 295-308.
Fincher, C. "The Proportions of Pluralism." *Research in Higher Education,* 1982, *17* (3), 283-285.
Franklin, P., and others. *Sexual and Gender Harassment in the Academy: A Guide for Faculty, Students, and Administrators.* New York: Modern Language Association, 1981.
Gartland, D., and Bevilacqua, N. "Sexual Harassment: Recent Research and Useful Resources." *Journal of the National Association for Women Deans, Administrators, and Counselors,* 1983, *46* (2), 47-50.
Gosman, E., and others. "Predicting Student Progression: The Influence of Race and Other Student and Institutional Characteristics on College Student Performance." *Research in Higher Education,* 1983, *18* (2), 209-236.
Hall, R., and others. *The Classroom Climate: A Chilly One for Women?* Washington, D.C.: Project on the Status and Education of Women, Association of American Colleges, 1982.
Hitt, M., Keats, B., and Purdum, S. "Affirmative Action Effectiveness Criteria in Institutions of Higher Education." *Research in Higher Education,* 1983, *18* (4), 391-408.
Jenkins, M. *Removing Bias: Guidelines for Student-Faculty Communication.* Annandale, Va.: Speech Communication Association, 1983.
Katz, J. "White Faculty Struggling with the Effects of Racism." In J. H. Cones, III; J. F. Noonan, and D. Janha (Eds.), *Teaching Minority Students.* New Directions for Teaching and Learning. San Francisco: Jossey-Bass, 1983.
McPherson, M. "Value Conflicts in American Higher Education: A Survey." *Journal of Higher Education,* 1983, *54* (3), 243-278.
Maihoff, N., and Forrest, L. "Sexual Harassment in Higher Education: An Assessment Study." *Journal of the National Association for Women Deans, Administrators, and Counselors,* 1983, *46* (2), 3-8.
Menges, R., and Exum, W. "Barriers to the Progress of Women and Minority Faculty." *Journal of Higher Education,* 1983, *54* (2), 123-144.
Metha, A., and Nigg, J. "Sexual Harassment on Campus: An Institutional Response." *Journal of the National Association for Women Deans, Administrators, and Counselors,* 1983, *46* (2), 9-15.
Panos, R. *Beyond Retention: A Survey of Black Alumni, Classes of 1972-1978.* Developmental Series. Oberlin, Ohio: Oberlin College, 1981.

Patton, M. Q. "Qualitative Methods and Approaches: What Are They?" In E. Kuhns, and S. V. Martorana (Eds.), *Qualitative Methods for Institutional Research,* New Directions for Institutional Research, no. 34. San Francisco: Jossey-Bass, 1982.

Peterson, M., and others. *Black Students on White Campuses: The Impacts of Increased Black Enrollments.* Ann Arbor: Survey Research Center, The University of Michigan, 1979.

Project on the Status and Education of Women. *Harvard Issues Statement About Sexual Harassment and Related Issues.* Washington, D.C.: Association of American Colleges, 1984a.

Project on the Status and Education of Women. *Sexual Harassment: A Summary Report.* Washington, D.C.: Association of American Colleges, 1984b.

Smith, D. *Admission and Retention Problems of Black Students at Seven Predominantly White Universities.* Washington, D.C.: National Advisory Committee on Black Higher Education at Black Colleges and Universities, Department of Education, 1980.

Terrass, S., and Pomrenke, V. "The Institutional Researcher as Change Agent." In J. Lindquist (Ed.), *Increasing the Use of Institutional Research,* New Directions for Institutional Research, no. 32. San Francisco: Jossey-Bass, 1981.

Thomas, G. E. (Ed.). *Black Students in Higher Education: Conditions and Experiences in the 1970s.* Westport, Conn.: Greenwood Press, 1981.

Verba, S., DiNunzio, J., and Spaulding, C. *Unwanted Attention: Report on a Sexual Harassment Survey.* Report to the Faculty Council of the Faculty of Arts and Sciences. Cambridge, Mass.: Harvard University, September, 1983.

James L. Litwin is director of Institutional Studies at Bowling Green State University in Ohio. He is cochair of the Ohio Association for Institutional Research, and currently serves on the Human Relations Commissions of the University and the City of Bowling Green.

Campuses should act on salary equity issues before litigation arises. Campuses must resolve data base problems, unfocused studies, problems in data interpretations, and constraints on implementing findings if they are to take timely actions.

Preparation, Prevention, and Response: Data Elements and Data Bases for Support

Celia Allard, Ira W. Langston, Frank A. Schmidtlein

Internally Motivated Monitoring

Institutional research offices are increasingly involved in efforts to supply data and conduct research on salary equity issues confronting campuses. This growing role is reflected in the proliferation of well-attended sessions on the topic at annual forums of the Association for Institutional Research. Data gathering and studies related to equity issues, if undertaken before serious controversy and litigation arises, can be accommodated to the work schedules of institutional research offices and made a part of decision-making processes with little disruption of the normal work flow, and with modest resources.

Once litigation is underway, demands for data and research are likely to overwhelm the institutional research offices, as well as other campus offices. Campus officials will have to devote a large portion of time to the litigation, leaving other important concerns unattended. Frequently, substantial costs for attorneys and experts are incurred. The conflict adversely affects campus morale, damages public relations, and creates an atmosphere that makes it difficult to reach a mutually agreeable solution to the problem.

After litigation begins, the parties can no longer communicate freely or engage in the candid discussions that are necessary to resolve any problems. Communications between the parties are made through attorneys. Attorneys generally take a conservative attitude toward providing information that could in any way strengthen an opposing attorney's position. Furthermore, though the faculty may continue to make its case public, the administration is restricted in what it may reveal. These circumstances impede reaching a negotiated settlement and raise suspicions about the good faith of both parties. In such an adversarial situation, it becomes nearly impossible to reconstruct accurate historical data.

Whatever evidence comes out of the reconstruction attempt may be used by either side, and a great deal is likely to come out. Many institutions have problems in obtaining reliable data. In "live" data systems, the data change continuously, so that if two people gain access to the same data file at different times, they may obtain two different answers, both of which would be correct (at the moment they are retrieved). Lawyers have not hesitated to request data from the institution in a volume and level of detail that is shocking to the layperson. These sweeping requests are intended to ferret out any data that are there to be found. If the institution relies on live data systems, or other less reliable sources such as memories, the data coming out at the time of a particular request may no longer be the original, correct data. Thus, it is easy to be put in a situation of having more than one set of data, with no way to prove which is accurate.

Faculty members often become suspicious and view the collaboration of administrators and attorneys as an attempt to rationalize unwarranted salary differences. Yet responsible administrators cannot address such complex issues, which potentially involve litigation, without sound advice. Attorneys give valuable advice on provisions of law and the legal precedents that set forth campus responsibilities. They frequently suggest improvements in the precision of the administration's language and make a substantial contribution to the clarity of statistical reports. Consequently, in addition to ethical considerations, a campus should have a strong practical interest in assessing salary inequities and acting on these assessments before serious problems emerge. Often, however, such action is not taken.

This section of the chapter examines four concerns that must be addressed in order to promote early campus attention to salary equity issues—to keep the campus out of the courtroom. These areas of concern are (1) the focus of salary equity research, (2) the interpretation of research findings, (3) the constraints on acting on findings, and (4) the character of the campus personnel data base. The second section of this chapter deals with data issues after a court finding has been made. Although there is some overlap, the focus and the activities differ.

The Focus of Faculty Salary Equity Research. The discovery of salary differences among faculty members who are similarly situated (in terms of such variables as years of professional experience, years since highest degree, rank, and productivity) is not completely helpful unless one can discover where in the salary-setting process unexplained differences occur. Similarly, studies that show differences in salary means between otherwise comparable classes of faculty members are not fully helpful unless a further process is available to discover which individuals are accounting for such differences and whether the differences are or are not justified. In order to overcome these problems, faculty salary studies must identify and separate the effects of each process that results in decisions on salary levels. These studies need to be followed up by an examination of the comparative salaries of similarly situated faculty members, in order to identify specific inequities and to make individual corrections. An across-the-board salary increase is not equitable if the salaries of some faculty members already match or exceed those of their similarly situated peers. Creating new inequities invites further litigation.

At a university, faculty salary levels are typically affected by three processes: First, salaries are established at the time faculty members are hired. Usually, initial salaries are arrived at by bargaining in the context of the faculty labor market in a given discipline. If an inequity occurs as a result of an initial employment decision, it can persist unless "catch-up" funds are subsequently provided. Therefore, one focus of salary studies should be initial employment salary-level decisions.

A second process that affects salary levels is annual, or periodic, reviews for awarding merit-based salary money, if any is available, and for providing across-the-board cost-of-living increases. Improper judgments can create inequitable awards of merit salary increments. Any existing salary inequities are magnified by percentage, across-the-board increases. Therefore, each effect of these processes needs separate examination.

A third process that can produce inequities is the salary decisions that accompany promotion and tenure reviews. Inequities in promotion decisions keep persons at a lower rank than their merit justifies, and this leads to improper selection of similarly situated faculty, if rank is used as a variable for comparisons. When favorable promotion and tenure decisions are made, salary increments that accompany these awards could be inequitable. Consequently, a thorough study of faculty salary equity must examine comparative promotion and tenure rates and salary awards that accompany such decisions. Separate studies of each of these salary decision-making processes can identify the origin of any unexplained differences and focus efforts on improving that specific process.

This brief discussion does not deal with the complexities of determining whether two faculty members are similarly situated. Neither does it deal with the methodologies for conducting research on faculty salary-setting processes. A description of how these issues were dealt with at the University of Maryland is contained in a paper by Brown and Schmidtlein (1984). The studies just described identify organizational units wherein average salary differences exist in order that further attention can be focused on them. They also track trends in average salary differences over time, identifying possible patterns. They further reveal the effects new appointments, promotions, pay raises, and terminations have on average salary differences. They do not, however, identify individual salary inequities. Therefore, a further salary review process is needed to identify and eliminate any individual inequities that might have arisen from a particular process.

There are many ways to design a faculty salary equity review process. The one employed at the University of Maryland at College Park (Brown and Schmidtlein, 1984) has the following chracteristics: The salary equity review process is made a part of the annual review used to award merit increases. Each of the five campus academic mandate affirmative action, Section 503, as amended, is an affirm- review the productivity and salary of each female faculty member in their division. The institutional research office supplies the review committees with faculty vita and computer generated listings of similarly situated male and female faculty members (that is, members of the same department, rank, and approximate number of years since obtaining highest degree). The committee assesses the comparative merit of each female and recommends to the provost what her salary level should be relative to her male comparison group. The provost compares these recommendations with the salary levels proposed by each department and makes any adjustments needed to maintain equity. The review also provides recommendations on adjustments in male faculty salary levels when indicated by the comparisons. This element is most important in the review of salary equity, since it both identifies and corrects any specific inequities. The statistical studies suggest areas for examination and identify trends, but they do not establish the existence of inequities or a basis for their correction. This limitation in statistical studies is not always perceived or appreciated by employees and the public.

The Interpretation of Research Findings. Reports of statistical studies have to address both lay audiences and critical researchers. Consequently, statistical formulas and technical terms must be explained simply and clearly enough to be understood by lay readers but must not lose their precision for researchers interested in methodology. This is a difficult balance to strike. Few readers find the results entirely satisfactory. Because of the sensitivity of such studies, statements not only have to be complete and accurate but also need to be interpreted accurately by readers. It is worthwhile to devote some effort to predicting the possible misinterpretations of statements.

Another balance that must be sought in writing reports is to reveal all possible conclusions about the data while at the same time wording findings so that they do not inadvertently provide opposing attorneys with evidence they may pull out of context to use against a campus. This is not a question of withholding or misinterpreting data, but of ensuring that an accurate balance is presented between adverse and positive findings, and also ensuring that these findings are placed in context. One area in which this problem will surface is in interpreting cumulative differences revealed in statistical salary studies. Usually one cannot conclude from such studies that differences are the result of discrimination (or, for that matter, that discrimination is not present), but it is very complex to explain why this is the case.

Another area subject to confusion is understanding why it is necessary to examine initial salary awards, annual salary increments, and promotion and tenure action effects on salary levels, in order to identify and locate any problems. Some faculty members argue that rank should not be a variable in a regression analysis of salary levels. However, failure to examine rank independently, through a promotion and tenure study, will limit one's ability to determine the extent to which each of the decision points contributes to any salary discrepancies. Traditionally, research reports tend to concentrate on what studies do reveal, rather than on what they do not reveal. For studies that might be used in legal proceedings, it is equally important to state clearly what one cannot conclude from findings.

Finally, many female faculty members presume that studies will reveal clear evidence of discrimination and that a failure to do so results from clever manipulation of data or incomplete presentation of facts. Administrators, on the other hand, frequently exhibit some need to justify past actions and presume that they have acted fairly. In order for research reports to be credible, they need to be as candid as possible with both the faculty audience and those administering salary decisions.

Constraints on Acting on Salary Equity Findings. There are a number of factors that inhibit campuses' attempts to take needed steps to prevent salary equity litigation. The first is the time and effort required of faculty and administrators to review the equity of salary, promotion, and tenure decisions. Some faculty and academic administrators see reviews of a female faculty member's salary level as time-consuming red tape added on to an already lengthy and cumbersome process.

Second, acting on findings can be viewed as an admission of guilt. The elimination of unjustified salary differences can be legally dangerous as well as ego bruising. However, failure to act only provokes existing forces for change and makes future resolution of problems more difficult.

Third, the publicity generated by studies of equity invariably focuses on negatives. One rarely gets a balanced interpretation of the situation. Past errors of judgment can be presented as conspiracies to create and maintain inequities. Consequently, administrators seek to avoid such adverse publicity. However, withholding information leads to further suspicion and lack of credibility. Generally one is better off to err on the side of openness.

Fourth, the advocates of most causes are not conservative in their statements or, occasionally, their demeanor. One rarely gets the public's attention by understating a case. Such advocacy frequently engenders a counter reaction. Administrators seek to avoid the appearance of "caving in" to intemperate demands and actions. Strength is sometimes needed to separate the merits of a case from the style and statements of its proponents.

Fifth, actions taken in response to studies are frequently viewed as circumventing established academic procedures. Furthermore, such actions often require additional time from faculty or staff and more paperwork. No one likes an added administrative burden, perhaps especially in institutions of higher education. However, the benefits of correcting any problems, especially if litigation is avoided, are worth a considerable effort.

Sixth, adjustments to female faculty salaries can be viewed as reverse discrimination by male faculty. Male faculty, and "unadjusted" female faculty can both view equity adjustments as reducing salary funds that might otherwise be applied to increase their own salary levels. This can engender a belief that faculty members are paying for the past sins of administrators and faculty salary committees. There is perhaps some truth to this charge, but unless one is able to get additional funds provided for salary equity, fairness requires using available funds for adjustments. Legislatures are not likely to reward public institutions for past transgressions by providing additional funds for adjustments. Finally, funds for salary equity adjustments may be taken from nonsalary sources in campus budgets. Those losing funds as a result of such decisions are likely to offer some resistance to equity actions.

The Campus Personnel Data Base. The personnel data bases at most institutions are constructed primarily to facilitate administrative operations, such as preparing the payroll, facilitating operational decisions, and preparing external statistical reports. The numbers used for most policy and planning processes are annual "snapshots" that contain personnel data from a particular date each fall. Salary equity studies, however, require comparable and highly accurate longitudinal personnel data. Unless the data base is designed specifically with such longitudinal use in mind and contains the data elements needed for such analyses, it will probably have significant limitations that are typically very expensive and time-consuming to correct. Even when an adequate data base is constructed, it is apt to contain high error levels unless it has been used as a basis for decisions and been subjected to the scrutiny that accompanies such use.

When a campus does not have a reasonably complete and accurate data base, salary equity studies will be highly time-consuming and expensive. Data problems are apt to be discovered incrementally while undertaking studies. At the University of Maryland, College Park, a promotion and tenure study that began as a six-month effort turned into a two-and-a-half-year project as a result of data errors and omissions. Consequently, it may make sense to design a new data base and begin accumulating data from the present, if the existing data base is inadequate, rather than trying to reconstruct history from old personnel files. Poor historical data does not preclude one from making current comparisons and acting on the results while a better data system is being developed.

The development and maintenance of a first-rate faculty data base is expensive. The costs are implicitly, if not explicitly, balanced by campuses against the uncertain future value of the data. This may account for the often neglected condition of these data bases. Good data have a very high value when campuses face the possibility of litigation. Data systems take time to develop before they can produce needed information. Therefore, institutions that have not addressed data problems may have an exceedingly difficult time defending themselves in court. A good personnel data base can help one prevent as well as respond more effectively to litigation.

Building a Longitudinal Data Base. At best, an equity support data base should span the longest possible period of time to ensure that historical patterns as well as new trends are captured by the data. In addition, since it is nearly impossible to determine in advance which data will be important, all data that might be important should be kept, including some that may not be currently collected. And finally, the selection of the data must be reliable and valid. There are certain times during the year that are important for determining who was on which contract, for example, and the data must reflect the actual official data at these times to be fully useful.

The perfect data base does not exist, and when the data are needed, one often finds that a few more years' worth of data or another variable would be appreciated, regardless of how diligently the data elements have been selected. Even so, it is far better to have a gap in a well-designed data base than to have no data base at all. And while the data base must be constructed and maintained within existing institutional constraints, it can be useful even if it is modest. If the data base is built carefully, with attention to the elements of litigation (see Chapter Three) there is a good chance it will serve a useful purpose.

Two or three years ago, the issue of who should create and maintain the data base would not have arisen. The administrative data-processing department would have been the only facility with access to the data and with the capability of building and maintaining a large data base. With the proliferation of such data manipulation systems as the Statistical Analysis System (SAS), high-powered microcomputers, and micro to mainframe linkages, many institutional research offices are fully capable of designing, building, and maintaining large longitudinal data bases. The merits of their doing so can only be discussed within the context of individual situations. However, those who use the data must weigh the advantages of ease of access, ease of design change, and quality control against the disadvantage of the extra workload involved. Some data-processing departments will resist giving up control of data base functions, but this situation, too, is changing rapidly.

If the primary purpose of the data base is to deal with discrimination and equity problems among faculty and staff, then the data stored in the system must do two things to be of value. First, the data must allow the identification of any faculty or staff group that might claim discrimination now or in the future. Second, the data must be as close to the actual data used in the decision making as possible, or it will run the risk of being judged irrelevant to the charge of discrimination. For example, if a faculty member claims to be paid less than other faculty members with less teaching skill and less experience and whose research is of lesser quality, and these are the factors used in rank and pay decisions, then the data base should provide accurate and objective measures of at least some of these factors.

The list of variables that might be important in the identification of disadvantaged groups or in determining discrimination are extensive but not infinite. Some key variables included in court cases have been sex; race; age; marital status; name, date, and area of concentration of highest aacademic degree; institution awarding highest degree; type, length, and original date of appointment; department; original and current salary; history of raises; original and current rank; date of each change of rank; and administrative appointments (past and present); measures of teaching, research, and service loads; and measures of teaching, research, and service merit. (Any teaching, research, and service variables must be related to data used in actual decision making and therefore will need to be defined in a manner compatible with the way the institution defines and uses them.)

In addition, certain summary data should be kept for each department. These data should include variables such as the total number of faculty members in the department; the demographics of the faculty; the number of faculty members at each rank; the average salary by rank; the number of tenured and nontenured faculty members; the number of faculty members in each year of the tenure track; teaching, research, and service loads of faculty members (by various breakdowns); and a record of which criteria were actually used for hiring, firing, and rank and pay decisions in each department, as well as how each faculty member was ranked on each criterion used. We recommend Batson's (1984) article on faculty data bases as a starting point for discussions of data elements to be included.

These data should be stored in a form as close as possible to that which is actually used in departmental decisions. In addition, faculty privacy must be maintained. This does not mean that faculty should not be able to see their own data or the data for their own or other departments. However, even if the data are coded, it is difficult to release data for individuals without disclosing the identification of those individuals. Thus, it is better to release departmental data in grouped form rather than in individual form with identification deleted.

The data should be as accurate as possible, and the faculty and staff should be given the opportunity to review and validate their own data on a routine basis. Such reviews may point out errors in the data, and it will certainly be more difficult to challenge the data later if individual faculty members have the opportunity to correct their own data and certify the correctness of that data in writing.

Court-Ordered Monitoring

Two decades' history of anti-discrimination legislation and litigation should provide sufficient incentive for colleges and universities to examine their employment statistics and take steps to eliminate any institutional discrimination they find. However, as the previous section of this chapter and the work of numerous authors indicate, such an investigation requires a commitment of time and money (see Brown and others, 1984; Batson, 1984; Yancey, 1982; Simpson and Rosenthal, 1982). A hard and often-repeated lesson is that such commitment is a good investment in employee relations, particularly if an audit keeps the institution out of court. This section will deal with data issues in the event that lawsuit results in a judgment against the institution.

Losing any lawsuit is damaging to a university. The publicity is destructive, the litigation costly, and tensions on campus are likely to be high. If the university loses a class-action suit brought on behalf of a large protected class, the costs of litigation and settlement may be burdensome and the policy changes divisive. In addition, the hidden cost of settlement will be the time and money required to generate the employment statistics used to monitor the court order. These issues differ enough from those just mentioned to warrant some discussion.

Court Assessment of the Situation. Once a discrimination case is lost, the court will issue an order to effect a settlement between the university and the plaintiffs. Terms of settlement will vary, of course, with the charges and the disposition of the court. By issuing an order for settlement, the court is trying to correct the conditions that led to discrimination; thus, the order reflects the court's opinion concerning the steps necessary to rectify the injustice.

Court Specifications. Court orders generally focus on both financial and policy reparations. The order may include an itemized list of very specific prescriptions for the institution, or it may be a much more general order for the litigants to negotiate their own settlement (Clark, 1977). Regardless of the specific provisions of the court order, if statistical arguments were used successfully against the university in court, statistical monitoring will probably be needed to demonstrate that the ordered settlement is having its intended effect. Responsibility for monitoring will presumably devolve to the campus institutional research office.

Typically, the institutional research office will have been involved in providing data to university attorneys throughout the suit, and institutional research personnel will be familiar with the university's side of the case. Once the court judgment is made, however, the case is closed, and the institutional research staff must focus on the problems as defined by the court order. Accepting the court's definitions and statistical techniques may prove difficult after focusing on the university's case for so long, but the adjustment is necessary if the institutional research office is to perform the monitoring function properly. The sooner the adversarial spirit can be squelched, the faster the university can move to repair the damage done by the suit.

The Monitoring System. The institutional research office will have to work closely with a number of other offices to set up a monitoring sytem, since modifications in university policy can have a profound effect on the monitoring process. Statistical monitoring in the absence of a policy context is meaningless because the necessary interpretive framework is lacking. The institutional research office should be privy to policy-setting discussions between the administration, the affirmative action office, and legal counsel.

Institutional research personnel are in the best position to offer advice concerning the statistical implications of suggested policy changes. Statistical implications should not direct the policies, however. A return to court is less likely if the university develops a decision-making process perceived as equitable by employees than if the reconciliation efforts are all directed toward building an airtight statistical monitoring sytem.

Before a suitable monitoring sytem can be developed, the institutional researchers must understand the court order thoroughly as well as the court's perception of the issues. A valuable first step in achieving this end is to review the court records of the case, particularly the arguments justifying the court decision. Another worthwhile tactic is to discuss the case with expert witnesses who testified at the trial, particularly the statistical expert for the plaintiffs, in order to better understand the statistical framework used to support the accusations of discrimination.

The role of the institutional research office in statistically monitoring the court settlement will depend on the extent to which statistical analysis of data figured in the court's decision and will depend on the implications of the court order for university policy. For a discrimination suit brought by an individual resulting in a settlement with no major policy implications, monitoring by the institutional research office is unnecessary. At the oppositie extreme, a class-action suit alleging disparate impact and won by a relatively large group (female faculty, for example) may well result in a settlement requiring elaborate statistical monitoring.

Establishing a Statistical Baseline. If statistical evidence played a major role in the trial, then the institutional research office should attempt to duplicate the statistical presentations made by the plaintiffs. This exercise should be undertaken before developing a monitoring tool and should use data that predates any court-mandated adjustments. Duplicating the plaintiffs' statistics establishes baseline figures to serve as a reference point for documenting progress toward the implementation of the court order. Duplicating plaintiffs' statistics can also offer considerable insight into the factors that the court judged relevant to the case and hence relevant to making policies fair and equitable.

Baseline Displays. Reproducing all the statistics introduced in the trial is certainly not necessary; a bewildering array of statistical arguments may have been presented in court. There will have been one or more key presentations, however, that turned the case in the plaintiffs' favor: Perhaps the tables originally presented as evidence for a prima facie case were never successfully countered, or a model developed during the course of the trial was accepted by the judge. The institutional research office should attempt to identify these key statistical presentations and duplicate them as closely as possible. A brief discussion with the plaintiffs' expert witness may be necessary to clarify definitions and procedures. For example, in a hiring case the university's definition of the pool of qualified applicants may differ significantly from the plaintiffs'. For monitoring purposes, the court-accepted definition must be used. In any case, the institutional research office should create a baseline as close to the plaintiffs' as possible. A wildly divergent baseline is not an auspicious starting point for documenting compliance with a court order.

Once the baseline statistics are established, new data reflecting court-ordered adjustments can be introduced into the data base and the statistics can be recalculated. In fact, this constitutes the simplest monitoring sytem: regular updating, recalculation, and comparison with an established baseline. If policy changes were mandated by the court order, these changes will have to be incorporated into the model before the statistics are recalculated. The institutional research office should take the responsibility for screening the data for errors, recalculating the statistics, and comparing the new results with earlier ones.

How soon the monitoring sytem should be run depends on the nature of the discrimination case. For example, monitoring hiring practices involving potential employees differs from monitoring promotion or salary practices involving current employees. The settlement for a case concerning hiring practices may require the university to employ the plaintiff immediately and revise the institution's hiring policies. There may be considerable lag before the effects of the new policies are felt, and the institution's demands for labor in the period following the settlement will be a major factor influencing this lag.

Using the System. Monitoring the effect of altered policies on current employees may yield faster results, especially if the court order includes a directive to review the disputed status of all members of the protected class. In this situatiion, the institutional research office first calculates the baseline statistics, immediately updates the data base with the changes resulting from the status review, and then recalculates the statistics using the updated information. The results of this calculation will be indicative of whether the changes made in employees' status had the effect intended by the court order. If the statistics still indicate that discrimination exists, the records of the protected class may have to be reexamined.

How often the system should be run also depends on the nature of the grievance. A system that monitors hiring practices may need to be run as often as once a month, while a system monitoring promotion or salaries need only be run as often as adjustments in those areas are made. Faculty members are generally reviewed for promotion annually, while promotions of classified staff occur throughout the year. Salaries are usually adjusted once a year.

Reports of the monitoring runs should be submitted regularly to the proper administrative authority and should probably be accompanied by a special warning from the institutional research office if the statistics show evidence of a potential discrimination problem. The report itself should be limited to the presentation of statistics and discussion of their implications; interpreting the success of anti-discrimination should be an administrative responsibility. The report should be brief, since wordy monographs tend to go unread. It should also be comprehensive, showing trends over time. Simple graphs or tables that track the monitoring statistic are particularly effective methods of presentation. A typical graph might track the percentage of minorities hired per month or the regression coefficient associated with being female in a salary model.

In addition to monitoring the test statistic, the institutional research office should take pains to present raw data, such as counts and percentages, in the report. Raw data serve as a reality check on statistics generated by a model and tend to stifle arguments from detractors who distrust data transformations or lack an understanding of statistical principles.

Modifying the System. Once the institutional research office has established an effective system of monitoring the court order, other offices on campus will probably want to extend or modify the system. A simple extension might be to monitor the same employement statistic for other protected groups. The court settlement may have resulted in policy changes and efforts to favor the winning class that could be interpreted as discriminatory by others. The institutional research office may succeed in forestalling a similar lawsuit by producing statistics that show that all protected groups are being treated equitably within the statistical framework sanctioned by the court.

As time passes, pressures to alter the monitoring system may mount. Changes may be necessitated by new university policies and state and federal laws, or changes may be suggested by those who perceive a way to "improve" the system. Improvements to the system that are not policy driven must be undertaken with great caution, for consistency with baseline statistics is essential in order to demonstrate progress over time. A desire to improve the model is quite understandable, but if little is gained from the suggested changes, it is better to avoid them rather than sacrifice comparability with baseline statistics.

If changes are made in the monitoring system, the institutional research office should run the old system concurrently with the new, at least until the new model generates enough statistics to establish a pattern. Old grievances die hard, and the university may well be faced with complaints from members of the plaintiffs' class long after the suit has been settled. If the institutional research office can show monitoring records collected since the settlement, these complaints may be circumvented—or at least reduced in scope to individual grievances.

If current monitoring is impossible, the institutional research office should establish a new statistical baseline and continue monitoring from that point, avoiding the temptation to compare new apples with old oranges. The institutional research office should document the changes made, including a thorough description of the conditions making the changes necessary and an honest appraisal of the impact of the changes on the monitoring sytem. Of course, this sort of disruption in the monitoring sytem should be avoided whenever possible.

The principal steps in monitoring a court order are researching the issues, isolating the essential statistics, establishing a statistical baseline, and maintaining comparability and consistency over time. The ultimate goal of the monitoring process is to be able to demonstrate that the chosen statistical indicator of discrimination is decreasing over time. In many tasks the institutional research office undertakes, the greatest pitfalls and complications have political origins rather than statistical ones. This is particularly true of the task of monitoring the court order.

References

Batson, S. W. "Developing Faculty Data Base and Institutional Research Studies as Advanced Planning Mechanisms for Potential Litigation." Paper presented at the annual Association for Institutional Research Forum, Fort Worth, Tex., 1984.

Brown, M. H., Schmidtlein, F. A., and Ochsner, N. L. "Sex Equity Research: Keeping the Campus Out of the Courtrooms." Paper presented at the annual Association for Institutional Research Forum, Fort Worth, Tex., 1984.

Clark, D. L. "Discrimination Suits: A Unique Settlement." *Educational Record,* 1977, Summer, 233-249.

Simpson, W. A., and Rosenthal, W. H. "The Role of the Institutional Researcher in a Sex Discrimination Suit." *Research in Higher Education,* 1982, *16* (1), 3-26.

Yancey, B. "The Role of the Institutional Researcher in Court Litigation: An Ounce of Prevention." Paper presented at the annual Association for Institutional Research Forum, Denver, Colo., 1982.

Celia Allard is research specialist in the Office of Institutional Research at Montana State University. She is currently involved in salary analyses of university faculty and state cooperative service agents. Her experience includes the monitoring of court-ordered remediation.

Ira W. Langston is coordinator of research and testing in the Office of School and College Relations at the University of Illinois. He is also an assistant professor of educational psychology. His research interests include salary equity, freshman performance, minority recruitment, admissions, and success.

Frank A. Schmidtlein is an assistant professor in the Department of Education Policy, Planning, and Administration at the University of Maryland, College Park. He served from 1980 to 1984 as assistant to the chancellor, monitoring and reviewing campus equity studies. He has conducted numerous workshops concerning the use of computers and statistics.

The notion that the heyday of discrimination lawsuits occurred in the late 1960s or early 1970s shows a clear lack of understanding of the laws and statutes directed toward discrimination. While the focus of such efforts may have changed, the potential for litigation has, if anything, greatly increased.

Responding to Litigation: The Roles and Strategies of Researchers in Court Cases

Bernard Yancey

Institutions of higher education are at risk with respect to litigation from a multitude of sources. The focus of this chapter, however, will be litigation that has arisen from claims of discrimination. It is primarily in such litigation that the evidence addressing these claims depends on the results of statistical analyses.

One of the most dangerous attitudes for an institution of higher education is that of complacency. Institutions of higher education are not sacrosanct. They may also have the perception that the heyday of discrimination lawsuits occurred during the late 1960s or early 1970s. Such a perception shows a clear lack of understanding of the laws and statutes directed toward discrimination. While the focus of such efforts may have changed, the potential for litigation has, if anything, greatly increased. Before researchers and administrators in higher education can fully understand the potential problems facing institutions, they need to take a closer look at the legal models for proof of discrimination and the statutes under which litigation can be brought.

Although an institution may have effectively implemented an affirmative action program and is apparently satisfying regulatory requirements, there are no guarantees that litigation will not occur. Institutions must not assume that a successful defense for claims of discrimination can be based solely on data they have collected and supplied to federal or state regulatory agencies. While this information may provide a starting point, it is seldom subjected to more than a cursory examination. It is the exception that probative statistical analyses are applied to this data and that the results are examined for patterns or trends over time. The institution that has developed an ongoing internal monitoring system that exceeds the requirements for reporting, including probative statistical analyses, is in a considerably better position with regard to litigation than those institutions without such systems; though having such a monitoring sytem does not guarantee that litigation will never occur.

The implementation of such a monitoring system is not nearly as costly as most institutions seem to believe. The costs involved are definitely less than can be accrued in the litigation process. Also, some institutions fail to realize that an ongoing internal monitoring system has far more benefits than merely acting as a safety system in the advent of a lawsuit. The information provided by such systems often provides pertinent data for personnel, management, and recruitment evaluation systems.

The first part of this chapter will be devoted to reviewing discrimination and the legal models of proof, along with the major statutes under which litigation claiming discrimination can be brought. The second part of the chapter will discuss the major events that occur in the litigation process, assuming that all remedies attempted prior to entering litigation have failed.

Discrimination and Models of Proof

Several basic theories have been proposed to describe the mechanisms involved in discrimination. One of the first of these was a model proposed by Thurow (1969), which views discrimination as a desire for monopoly of power. A second theory stressed by Becker (1971) concentrates on personal prejudice, and a third concentrates on role prejudice (Boulding, 1976). While these theories are proposed as major components of discrimination, it should be recognized that discrimination is a complex phenomenon, occurring at almost any stage in a social process, and it has yet to be fully explained. Boulding (1976) provides a brief overview that should furnish a starting point for the interested reader and aid in understanding the complexities and potential impact of discrimination. The question of the existence of discrimination is a legal question, and there are no absolute or foolproof tests (statistical or otherwise) that can determine whether discrimination exists. There are, however, several legal models of proof that can be used as guidelines.

Facial Discrimination. The first model to be discussed will be facial discrimination. Under such a model, the claim is made that on the face of it a rule discriminates because it classifies individuals based on a particular set of characteristics; for example, "no blacks need apply" or "males only." Under such a model, all the claimant must do is demonstrate that he or she is disadvantaged by the rule (Tribe, 1978). It is doubtful that the researcher will be confronted with such a model. However, the potential still exists, particularly in such areas as the participation of women in traditionally all-male intercollegiate sports.

Disparate Treatment. The second model is labeled disparate treatment. Discrimination under this model is also sometimes referred to as intentional discrimination. The claim under such a model is that the defendant covertly favors one group of individuals over another due to membership in the group. Such a claim alleges intentional, purposeful discrimination in either a rule-making or rule-applying context. The applicability of this model depends on whether the claim of discrimination is being brought by an individual or by a group or class of individuals. Under a classwide injury model, the goal is to prove that an entire group of individuals has been intentionally discriminated against. It is not necessary to prove that members of the group are totally excluded or always treated less favorably or that discrimination against any one individual actually exists, but only that the overall policy is biased. Under the individual claimant model, the question is whether one individual has been discriminated against because of his or her group status.

Under the model of disparate treatment, if the plaintiff establishes a prima facie case of discrimination by demonstrating that the defendant could have exercised discretion and by offering qualitative testimony on the treatment of individual members and statistical evidence showing disproportionate treatment, then the burden shifts to the defendant to prove that the observed, disproportionate treatment was caused by legitimate circumstances (Baldus and Cole, 1980.)

Disparate Impact. The third model is disparate impact. The claim under such a model is that criteria and procedures are being used that significantly burden members of protected groups. Furthermore, these procedures and criteria and the unequal results they produce cannot be proven rationally related to the job or outcome. It should be noted that under the disparate treatment model, the intent is also irrelevant and the sole concern is the impact on the affected group. Also, under such a model, the defendant may justify criteria and procedures by demonstrating that they are job related.

To establish a prima facie case under the model of disparate impact, the plaintiff must demonstrate that the rule or procedure under question produces a substantial disproportionate impact. Because of the nature of the claim, the proof is almost always quantitative. Under the model of disparate impact statistical evidence is not merely circumstantial, as it is for the model of disparate treatment, but it is concerned with direct evidence that demands additional justification. When proof is of a statistical nature, the burden is usually on the plaintiff to demonstrate that the observed occurrences did not happen by chance. Not only must a substantial disproportionate impact be demonstrated, but this difference must be shown to be statistically significant (Baldus and Cole, 1980). Once the plaintiff establishes that substantial disproportionate impact exists, then the burden of proof shifts to the defendant to demonstrate that the criteria in question are legitimate and job related.

Statutes Under Which Claims May Be Filed

The following brief descriptions of the various statutes under which claims may be filed are not intended to be comprehensive in any sense, legal or otherwise, but only to give the reader a sense of their intent. Also, the list is not intended to be complete, but only representative. It is likely that the original acts have been amended, and the reader is encouraged to seek information on the current status of the statutes including any amendments and interpretations of enforcement policies, from appropriate legal counsel.

The Civil Rights Act of 1866 and 1971. This act has several sections. Section 1981 of the act is often seen as providing equal rights under the law and is uniformly interpreted by the courts as prohibiting racial discrimination in private employment (Strickler, 1979). Strickler (p. 103) also notes that while "section 1981 and Title VII of the 1964 Civil Rights Act overlap in providing remedies against racial discrimination in employment, there is no bar to using both at the same time." Section 1982 provides that all citizens have the same rights with respect to the inheritance, purchase, leasing, selling, holding, and conveying of real or personal property. Section 1983 provides for civil action in the event of deprivation of these rights, and in *Jones v. Alfred H. Mayer Co.* (392 U.S. 409 [1968]), the Supreme Court held that Section 1983 prohibits private acts of racial discrimination in the sale or rental of housing (Strickler, 1979). Section 1985 provides for civil action against one or more members of a conspiracy that is construed to deprive an individual or individuals of their civil rights. Section 1988 authorizes the federal court to extend common law, as modified by the Constitution and acts of Congress, to afford relief in civil rights cases when relief under federal statutes may be insufficient (Strickler, 1979).

Title VII. Title VII of the *Civil Rights Act of 1964* (U.S. Bureau of National Affairs), prohibits discrimination based on race, color, religion, sex, or national origin. Sections 703 and 704 spell out specifically prohibited employment practices, while Section 705 allows for the creation of the Equal Employment Opportunity Commission. Section 703 (a) states: "It shall be an unlawful employment practice for an employer (1) to fail or refuse to hire or to discharge any individual, or otherwise to discriminate against any individual with respect to his compensation, terms, conditions, or privileges of employment, because of such individual's race, color, religion, sex, or national origin; or (2) to limit, segregate, or classify his employees or applicants for employment in any way that would deprive or tend to deprive any individual of employment opportunities or otherwise adversely affect his status as an employee, because of such individual's race, color, religion, sex, or national origin." Section 703 (b) extends these prohibitions to labor unions and organizations. Section 704 extends these prohibitions to access to on-the-job training, apprenticeship programs, or other training programs.

Title VI. Title VI of the *Civil Rights Act of 1964* (p. 115) specifies in Section 601: No person in the United States shall, on the grounds of race, color, or national origin, be excluded from participation in, be denied the benefits for, or be subjected to discrimination under any program or activity receiving federal financial assistance." Section 602 empowers each federal department and agency to provide such assistance to enforce the provisions specified under Section 601.

The Equal Pay Act. The *Equal Pay Act of 1963* (Sec. 206 d), is an amendment to the *Fair Labor Standards Act of 1938* (Sec. 201, et seq.). The basic prohibitions of this act, according to Strickler (1979, p. 108), are as follows: "discrimination in wages or rates of pay between employees doing equal work on jobs, the performance of which requires equal skill, effort, and responsibility, and which are performed under similar working conditions, because of sex (wage differentials based on systems of seniority, merit, quantity or quality of production, or on any factor other than sex are not prohibited)." The liability of this act extends to any employer covered by the *Fair Labor Standards Act* or any labor organization causing or attempting to cause violations of the act.

The Age Discrimination in Employment Act of 1967. This act and the Additional Provisions of the *Age Discrimination in Employment Act Amendments of 1978* form the basis of claims of age discrimination. These acts prohibit discrimination based on age with respect to hiring, discharge, compensation, terms, conditions, or privileges of employment. They further prohibit limiting, segregating, or classifying employees in any way with respect to age that would adversely affect their status as employees. These prohibitions are extended to employment agencies and labor organizations. The acts also prohibit the printing or publishing of any employment notice indicating any preference, limitation, specification, or discrimination based on age. The provisions of the *Act of 1967* are limited to those individuals who are at least forty years of age but less than seventy years of age. They do not prohibit the compulsory retirement of individuals who are between the ages of sixty-five and seventy occupying bona fide executive or high policy-making positions or working under a contract of unlimited tenure at an institution of higher education.

The Rehabilitation Act of 1973. Section 501 of the *Rehabilitation Act of 1973* prohibits discrimination based on handicapped status in the federal sector. The interpretation of this act is extended to those individuals or agencies that are receiving federal funds.

Section 504 mandates equal opportunity and nondiscrimination in employment, prohibiting discrimination based on handicap in all employment actions, decisions, policies, and practices. As a result, recipients (of federal money) must not only ensure an absence of discrimination against qualified handicapped persons, but also must make adjustments and accommodations in individual instances to make certain that equal opportunities exist for qualified handicapped applicants and employees. While Section 504 does not mandate affirmative action, Section 503, as amended is an affirmative action statute. This separate law is administered by the U.S. Labor Department and is applicable to all federal (sub)contractors with (sub)contracts of $2,500 or more.

Strengths and Weaknesses of the Positions

There are several inherent strengths and weaknesses for both the defendant and plaintiff in a litigation process that centers around the use of statistical analyses. In such a situation, the defendant uses the results of statistical analyses to refute the claims made by the plaintiff, while the plaintiff uses similar analyses to establish the prima facie case. To begin with, there are no standard or "cookbook" strategies for using statistical analyses, either for the defendant or for the plaintiff. While certain rules of thumb are often used by the courts, such as the "4/5's rule" or the "2 or 3 standard deviation rule," such rules of thumb often have little or no foundation in statistical theory. Their use generally serves to demonstrate a clear lack of understanding of the statistical concepts involved.

For the results of the statistical analyses to be meaningful, the choice of analyses is dependent first on the characteristics, quality, and quantity of the data, and second on the questions or claims that have been raised. With this in mind, the plaintiff has a wide range of strategies to use to establish the prima facie case. The plaintiff can, in essence, take any approach that will benefit his or her case most. It is up to the defendant to anticipate and defend against such approaches.

The plaintiff who depends solely on compliance with state or federal guidelines as a means of defense in the litigation process is in for a shock. The plaintiff's approach will not, in all likelihood, be based on any of the data gathered to evaluate degree of compliance with mandated guidelines. In general, the accuracy of much of the data collected to monitor compliance, such as that contained on EEO-1 or EEO-6 forms, is often considered suspect by the courts. While anticipating the plaintiff's strategy may seem an impossible task, the acquisition of such information should be one of the primary goals of the defendant in the discovery portion of the litigation process. The degree of advantage for the plaintiff depends on the resources he or she has available. Given a capable expert and adequate computer resources and staff, there are a considerable number of approaches that the plaintiff can take for any given set of claims.

However, in litigation that is dependent on statistical analyses and thus on data, the defendant does have one advantage. In most instances, the data on which the statistical analyses are to be performed to establish the prima facie case can only be obtained from the defendant through discovery. This is also the case for any elaborating information that may be needed by the plaintiff to help understand the data that have been provided. The defendant probably has immediate access to the data and individuals who maintain and update the data. If the defendant has appropriately structured files and has kept the needed data, the defendant's staff should be able to perform and summarize analyses much more quickly and thoroughly than could the plaintiff. The most common mistake made by defendants, however, it the failure to keep enough data to defend themselves. (See Chapter Two of this volume for further discussion of this point.)

Putting Together the Team

The defense of an institution in the litigation process requires a team approach. One such team approach might consist of four basic subgroups coordinated by individuals from the following four areas: the administration, the legal staff, the decision support group, and the experts. The makeup of these subgroups and their responsibilities might be as follows:

The Administration. The representative from the administration should be in a position to guarantee that adequate resources can be allocated for the defense of the institution. These resources include the cooperation of those individuals inside the institution who are needed to prepare its defense. The representative should be able to work closely with the university attorney or attorneys and be actively involved in all decisions concerning the process that are not of a strictly legal nature. Care must be taken that the representative does not become bogged down in the details of the process but maintains an overall view of the situation. Hopefully, this individual will have a working knowledge of the capabilities and limits of the resources and individuals that may be needed.

The Legal Staff. The attorney is in charge of the legal aspects of the case. It is his or her responsibility to communicate legal issues to the administration and support personnel in an accurate and timely fashion. Any communication between the attorney and an employee of the institution is considered privileged, while communications with the attorney and outside experts are not and are subject to discovery. Even with the attorney-client privilege, it is recommended that communications with the attorney be primarily of an oral nature.

Equal employment opportunity litigation is complex, both from a legal point of view and because so much of the evidence is of a statistical nature. Therefore, if an equal employment opportunity suit is brought against an institution, and university attorneys do not have equal employment opportunity litigation experience, an attorney with such experience should be sought out and brought in. In communicating the legal aspects of the case, the attorney must provide and explain enough information to allow the institution to gather statistical data needed for its defense, while being careful not to bury the support personnel in the legal subtleties of the case.

One hopes that the attorney will have had experience in cases using statistical data and will be able to work with the support personnel and the outside expert. An institution may have the statistical evidence to defend itself, but the attorney must have the skills to use this evidence in order for it to be effective.

The attorney should have a working knowledge of the problems and limitations involved when using statistical analyses as evidence and use all legal means available to ensure that the institution has adequate time to perform the analyses needed for its defense.

The Decision Support Group. This group is made up of several individuals. The individual in charge, however, if not a statistician, should have extensive institutional research experience. Furthermore, this individual should be one who can effectively communicate with the administration, the institution's attorney, and the outside expert. The following skills are critical in the decision support group and if not present in the individual in charge, should be found in other members of the group:

1. Extensive experience in building data bases where the sole purpose is the generation of statistical analyses. Very few individuals from a strict data processing background have either the skills or the orientation to accomplish such a task effectively.

2. A thorough knowledge of the personnel policies and practices of the institution pertaining to the individuals involved. If the claims involve students, then an individual with a thorough working knowledge of admissions policies, grading policies, and so forth should be involved.

3. A thorough working knowledge of the location and contents of personnel documents, payroll files, and so on. If such infor-

mation exists in a computer printout format, then this individual should know where and how this information is stored. One of the members of the decision support group should probably be the individual or individuals who maintain such files.

4. A thorough working knowledge of the computer resources available, including hardware and software.

5. A working knowledge of statistical designs and methods that have been used in litigation, including the advantages and limitations of each approach. This individual should have a broad enough knowledge of statistical methods and approaches to apply approaches that may be applicable but that have not been traditionally used in litigation.

6. A working knowledge of the statistical models of proof often used in litigation.

7. The ability to summarize the results of statistical analyses, including the generation of charts and graphs, and the ability to communicate this information to individuals with no background in the area. Skills in this area are of prime importance.

The Expert. If litigation occurs and a statistical expert is needed, someone from outside the institution should be hired, particularly if the litigation involves a jury trial. Testimony from an individual who is being paid by the institution will seldom be considered nonpartisan either by a judge or by a jury.

When choosing an outside expert, the following points should be kept in mind. There are two general ways of using an outside expert. One is to use the expert to communicate the results of statistical analyses to the court, while the other is to use the expert as a pawn in the game of resume comparisons. The defendant who employs an expert simply to communicate the results of statistical analyses to the court is in a considerably better legal position that the defendant who bases the defense on the expert's opinions, which are primarily supported by the expert's past experience and credentials and are not soundly based on the results of statistical analyses.

While the past litigation experience of a potential expert is of great importance, other factors should be considered simultaneously when hiring an expert. These include working style, communication skills, and the ability to work as part of a team. The defense of an institution is a team effort and is seldom won or lost on the efforts of a single individual. However, glaring statistical errors or omissions evidenced in past work of the expert in a litigation setting should not be overlooked. Caution should be used when considering an expert whose primary source of income is through work as an expert witness. An individual who works only part-time as an expert and has primary employment in another setting, academic or otherwise, will be more credible in a courtroom setting. Also, any statistician who has testified or is willing to testify to the presence or absence of discrimination should be considered with extreme caution. The presence or absence of discrimination is a legal, not a statistical question. The statistician can only testify to the presence or absence of statistically significant differences between groups.

The expert must work with the institution's attorney to outline the information needed to defend the institution. This includes anticipating the analytic strategy that will be employed by the plaintiff. Communications between the expert and the institution's attorney and any employees of the institution are subject to discovery and should thus be exercised with discretion.

Since the expert is the one presenting the actual testimony, it is best if the expert designs the analysis strategy and the exhibits used in the presentation. This strategy should be developed using input from the institution's attorney, the representative from the administration, and the decision support group.

While the expert-attorney interaction is of great importance, the interaction between the expert and the decision support group is critical. It is the decision support group that the expert must rely on for the data needed to defend the institution. One of the primary responsibilities of the expert and the decision support group is to ensure that all the implications and ramifications of the data supplied to the plaintiff via discovery are known before the information is supplied; or to be more specific, that no surprises occur.

Timing. Ideally, given the potential that an institution has for becoming involved in litigation, a team such as the one just described should exist well in advance of any actual litigation. If an internal monitoring sytem is in place, then the individuals responsible for the system could and probably would form the core of the team. In the absence of such a core group, the team should be formed at the time a complaint is filed. With respect to equal employment opportunity cases, this should occur when the complaint is filed with the Equal Employment Opportunity Commission. It is not absolutely necessary to bring in an outside expert at this point, but a list of prospective individuals should be compiled. When litigation becomes a certainty, however, an outside expert should be sought immediately.

The time period after a claim has been filed and prior to the start of litigation should be used by the administration, legal staff, and decision support group to identify the data, individuals, and resources needed to refute the claim and to defend the institution if litigation is brought. If internal self-assessment is not ongoing, then this would be the appropriate time to build the various data bases that will be needed (separately from existing production data bases). This is also the time to complete a thorough analysis of the various data relevant to the claim that is being made. Hopefully, such analyses are being conducted on an ongoing basis. If even the core of the team exists as part of an ongoing monitoring system, then gearing up for a full-fledged defense effort is considerably easier than if the team must be pulled together from scratch.

Stages of Litigation and Some Appropriate Strategies

Discovery

One critical stage in the litigation process is discovery. At this stage the court will require the defendant to provide data or information to the plaintiff to allow the plaintiff to try to establish a prima facie case. The court will often require the defendant to provide the plaintiff with copies of personnel documents and records. The plaintiff will file interrogatories for requests for production or both, asking for answers to a series of questions or requesting that specific documents be produced. The plaintiff may take a series of legal steps to delay or prevent the release of some or all of the requested documents and information. During this same time period the defendant may also submit interrogatories to the plaintiff. While the purpose of discovery may be quite different, depending on the viewpoint of the plaintiff or the defendant, the basic sequence of events is often the same.

The sequence of events in discovery often begins with opposing sides taking the depositions of key individuals in the litigation. The plaintiff's attorneys will attempt to identify the nature and location of key personnel documents, find out which individuals are in decision-making positions, and so forth, while the defendant's attorney will attempt to determine the exact nature of the claims that have been made. The information derived from the depositions will then be used to structure the interrogatories and requests for production. Discovery usually occurs for a limited time period. The length of time can often be influenced by the attorneys for either side and can be a critical factor in the outcome of the case.

The Plaintiff's Primary Objectives. The primary objectives of the plaintiff during discovery are as follows:

1. Identify and obtain copies of all personnel documents and records, either in their raw form or via the use of statistical analysis, that could be used to provide support for the claims that have been raised. With respect to documents, this would involve not only determining whether or not they exist but also how they are stored. Is the information stored on paper documents or in a computer readable format? An outline of the specific types of documents and information that can be requested is included at the end of this chapter and is titled "A Plaintiff's Discovery Checklist."

2. Identify individuals within the institution who are in key decision-making positions and who could have influenced the plaintiff and contributed to the claims being raised.

3. Determine what resources the institution can use to defend itself. What kind of computer resources and personnel does the institution have? What is the commitment of the institution's administration? Have adequate resources been allocated, or can they be allocated in terms of money and personnel? Has the institution hired an outside expert? Has the institution successfully defended itself in similar litigation in the past?

4. Determine whether or not there are additional individuals at the institution whose circumstances may be similar to the plaintiff's and who could thus join in the suit.

5. Attempt to discover what strategy or strategies the defendants and their expert will employ in defense of the institution.

6. Assess the validity of the plaintiff's claims. What hard evidence in the form of personnel documents, payroll records, and so forth exists that would support the claims made by the plaintiff?

The Defendant's Primary Objectives. The defendant's primary objectives during discovery should be the following:

1. Assess the resources available to the plaintiff for conducting the lawsuit. Does the plaintiff have access to qualified experts, computer resources, computer and clerical personnel, and so forth? If the litigation involves statistical analyses, how quickly can the plaintiff collect and analyze the data?

2. Determine the strategy or strategies to be employed. This would include determining both the legal strategies to be employed by the plaintiff's attorneys and the data analysis strategies to be employed by either the institution or its expert.

3. Determine the content and quality of the testimony to be given by the plaintiffs.

While the objectives just enumerated may be the most obvious ones, both sides will also usually have a series of hidden objectives. During the discovery process, the plaintiff's attorneys will attempt to determine through an examination of the information obtained whether or not additonal evidence exists, not necessarily related to the case at hand, that could be used to file additional suits against the institution. For example, an equal employment opportunity case may have been filed, initially alleging discrimination based on national origin, but the plaintiff's attorneys may discover during the discovery process that ample evidence exists to support a claim of sex discrimination. To be quite candid, filing multiple lawsuits can be an effective strategy to induce the institution to settle outside of court as a means of limiting cost. Given this possibility, it cannot be stressed enough that the defendant should not surrender any data or information during the discovery process until the data have been thoroughly analyzed by the members of the decision support group at least and, if possible, by the outside expert.

To be more specific, with respect to the information supplied in response to the interrogatories, the following points should be kept in mind:

1. The analyses and summaries that have been prepared should speak only to the questions that have been raised in the interrogatory, no more and no less.

2. The summaries should be carefully reviewed and approved by the attorney and the administrative official in charge before they are released.

3. While the institution may be obliged to provide answers to the interrogatories to the best of its ability, the final decision about the format of the response lies with the attorney and the administrative official in charge of the case.

4. The responses provided to the interrogatories are evidence and can be used in the litigation proceedings, either at the class certification stage or at the actual trial. Great care should thus be taken to ensure their accuracy and prevent them from contracting other results that may be presented.

5. The summaries should not contain any opinions, interpretations, or statements of implication about the results.

One approach taken by defendants in the past, but with decreasing success and thus, strongly cautioned against here, is to bury the plaintiff in documents and information during discovery, while pushing for an early trial. This approach assumes that the plaintiff will simply not have the time and resources to adequately analyze the data and prepare for the trial. While this may have been a valid strategy five to ten years ago, the advent of cheap computer power and the increasing knowledge of how to use it, particularly among members of the legal profession, has caused the dangers in such an approach to clearly outweigh the potential benefits. The plaintiffs should only be supplied with the information that is requested.

If information derived during discovery indicates that the plaintiffs may have some difficulty collecting and analyzing the data that is needed to support the claims they have made, then by all means a legitimate legal strategy would be to push for an early trial date and limit the preparation time available. Adequate time, however, should be planned to ensure that the decision support group and the expert retained by the institution are prepared for the trial. If an internal ongoing monitoring sytem exists at the institution, the time needed for this preparation is minimized.

Pre-Trial Preparation During Discovery. While the plaintiff's time will be consumed with the collection and analysis of data obtained during discovery, the defendant should use this time for data analysis to determine whether the claims of the plaintiff can be supported. If an internal ongoing monitoring system is in place, then the number of analyses that must be performed at this stage is greatly reduced and a large portion of the defendant's efforts can be saved for mapping strategies and developing methods of presentation.

The defendant's use of time during discovery is critical. The defendant should thoroughly review all analyses pertaining to the litigation. This point is particularly important with respect to the data that have been provided to the plaintiff during discovery. There are few situations more embarrassing and potentially damaging than that of having a plaintiff's expert testify to obvious idiosyncrasies, inconsistencies, and implications contained in an institution's personnel or payroll records, which the institution's expert and staff cannot explain and are apparently unaware of.

Class Certification

The importance of this stage in the litigation process should not be overlooked. At this stage the potential expenses and damages that may have to be paid by an institution can be minimized. If the "class" is certified, then the potential costs to the institution can be increased dramatically. The roles of the decision support group and the expert are of prime importance at this stage, given that the preponderance of the evidence presented will be of a statistical nature.

Defining the Class. Under a classwide injury model, the contention is that the members of a particular group are more likely to be injured by means of discrimination because of their membership in the group. The legal basis of the litigation rests on the inclusion of these groups as "protected groups" as defined by the statutes that have been discussed earlier. For example, if the claim is one of sex discrimination, then the proposed class of individuals could be all the female employees who were employed by an institution during a specified time period. Under such a model it is not necessary to show that all members of the class were discriminated against or always treated less favorably, but rather to support the inference that discrimination was the defendant's "standard operating procedure, the regular rather than the unusual practice" *(International Brotherhood of Teamsters* v. *United States,* 1977, p. 336). Proof of direct discrimination against any one individual is not required, but rather support must be found for an inference that the overall policy or practice is biased.

In the past, under a classwide injury model as defined by such cases as *Hazelwood School District* v. *United States* and *Castaneda* v. *Partida* (1977) the basic requirements for the plaintiff to establish the prima facie case were as follows:

The plaintiff had to first show that the defendant had the discretionary power to make the decisions or implement the policies that were being alleged to differentially impact the members of the class. After this had been done, the plaintiff had to offer qualitative testimony concerning the treatment of individual class members along with statistical evidence designed to show a disproportionate impact on the protected class. The degree of this disproportionate impact was also addressed in *Castaneda* and *Hazelwood,* and resulted in the development of the "2 or 3 standard deviation rule," which is one of the "rules of thumb" most often used by the courts and members of the legal profession for determining whether or not a difference is statistically significant. The potential for misuse and misinterpretation using this rule should be obvious to anyone with a reasonable exposure to statistical theory. For a more comprehensive discussion of the problems associated with statistical tests currently used in Title VII discrimination cases, see Bien and Santangelo (1982).

The legal requirements for establishing the existence and certification of a class will most likely vary depending on the specific claims that have been raised. This situation emphasizes the importance of the attorney's role in communicating the legal requirements of the case to the decision support group and the expert. For example, the certification of a class under Title VII may have been more strictly defined and restricted by *General Telephone Co. of the Southwest v. Falcon* (1982). The opinion issued in this case states that individual litigants seeking to maintain a class action must meet the prerequisites of numerosity, commonality, typicality, and adequacy of representation specified in the Federal Rule of Civil Proceedings 23.

Strategies. In general, at the class-certification stage the plaintiff attempts to show that the defendant had the discretionary power to make the decisions that could have produced the alleged effects of discrimination. Once the discretionary power of the defendant is established, then the plaintiff attempts to demonstrate, usually through the use of qualitative testimony and statistical evidence, the existence of a disproportionate impact on or treatment of members of the class. Once this has been acomplished, the plaintiff's next goal is to identify the members of the affected class. This is normally done by generating a list of individuals who have either shared or have the potential for sharing the injury with other members of the class.

The plaintiff needs only to establish the prima facie case, and then the burden shifts to the defendant. There are several strategies open to the defendant at the class-certification stage.

Discretionary Power. One of the first possible strategies involves attacking the claims of the plaintiff that the policies or practices alleged to be causing the observed disproportionate impact are due to discretionary decisions made and policies implemented by the defendant. For example, if the question is one of hiring, then the defendant may be able to demonstrate that any disproportionate representation in the employee base may be due to disproportionate availability in the available work force. It may also be that this disproportionate representation is aggravated or induced by state or federal regulations. In other words, the defendant would seek to show that the practices and policies in question were forced on the institution.

The Statistical Evidence. Whenever statistical evidence is presented, there are at least two avenues of attack to consider when countering the evidence. The first of these centers around the quality, accuracy, and completeness of the data on which the analyses are performed; the second concentrates on the actual statistical methods used.

The quality, accuracy, and completeness of the data used in the statistical analyses are of prime importance. At this point in the process, the defendant's easy and more immediate access to data can be put to greatest advantage. The specific strategy of the defendant, however, depends on just how accurate and complete the data are and how completely the defendant analyzed the data that was turned over to the plaintiff during discovery.

Once the defendant's data are of reasonable quality, accuracy, and completeness, and the defendant's staff has done its homework, careful attention must be paid to how the plaintiff interprets the data and the results of the analyses performed on the data. It is quite possible that the plaintiff and plaintiff's expert may misinterpret the data simply because they do not possess all the information in the possession of the defendant as to how the data were collected, maintained, and so forth. Such apparently minor information as changes in coding schemes or times and methods of data collection can dramatically affect the interpretation of statistical analyses.

If the data to be analyzed are of sufficient quantity to justify the use of computers, and if the data are not supplied to the plaintiff in a computer printout format, then the data must be converted into a computer printout format. This is a time-consuming and tedious task. Once the data have been converted to a computer printout format, the resulting computer files must be verified against the original documents to ensure accuracy. This task should not be attempted by individuals with no experience in building data files for performing statistical analyses. A multitude of steps must be taken in this process, and the omission of any one can produce a data set of questionable accuracy that will result in erroneous statistical analyses.

A point of caution should be noted. It may be that both the data in the possession of the defendant and the data supplied to the plaintiff are of questionable quality. The defendant may be tempted to attack the findings of the plaintiff, alleging that the quality of the data is such that nothing can be proved based on analyses performed on the data. Such a strategy is a double-edged sword. If nothing can be proved based on the data, then neither can anything be disproved. In using such a strategy, the defendant may create a situation of having no data left on which to base a defense.

If the data or data preparation cannot be or is not successfully attacked, then the next strategy might be to attack the analyses performed by the plaintiff or the plaintiff's expert. But unless some obvious errors are made by the plaintiff or the plaintiff's expert, the case may come to rest on which of the experts is most believable.

When considering the statistical analyses performed by the plaintiff, there is often a discussion of appropriate or inappropriate statistical methodology or tests. Strictly speaking, it is not the statistical methodology or tests that are appropriate or inappropriate, but rather, the interpretation of these methods or tests. Also, most experienced practitioners consider statistics more an art than a science, and if they look to the courts for guidance as to the appropriate interpretation of analyses, they will be sadly disappointed. Unfortunately, the majority of the statistical rules of thumb that are currently being used by the courts are overly susceptible to misuse and misinterpretation.

Miscellaneous Strategies. Depending on the local rules, the court, and the understanding among the attorneys, an attempt may be made to prevent any of the witnesses in the case, including the respective experts, from hearing the testimony given by some or all of the other witnesses. While the seclusion of witnesses may have some intuitive appeal, with respect to the experts, at both the class-certification stage and the actual trial such intuitive appeal can best be described as myopic. The respective experts should be allowed to hear the testimony of all the witnesses. The fields of law and statistics are both extremely broad and complex. It is rare to find an individual who is a functional expert in both areas. While the attorney is listening to testimony to understand the legal implications, the statistician or expert must hear the testimony to determine its statistical implications. While the strategies employed by the plaintiff's expert may not depend on the initial testimony of the plaintiff's witnesses, the strategy of the defendant's expert is closely linked to the testimony given by the plaintiff's witnesses.

The Trial

If no settlement can be reached, and the case actually goes to trial, the trial itself may be rather anti-climactic. The strategies employed by the plaintiff may be a continuation of those used at the class-certification stage or the tactics may be totally changed. The basic strategies for countering the approach of the plaintiff are basically the same for the defendant as at the class-certification stage, unless the class was not certified. The basic contested issues should have been identified.

Strategies. If a class was not certified, then the model of proof becomes one sometimes described as the "individual claimant model" (Baldus and Cole, 1980).

Under an individual claimant model the focus of the use of statistical evidence changes. When a class is being considered, groups of individuals are being compared. The use of statistics under the class model more closely resembles the traditional use of statistics for comparing groups. Under an individual claimant model one strategy is to compare the plaintiff or plaintiffs to some standard group of employees. This may be, for example, all other employees employed at the same time as the plaintiff with similar qualifications, training, experience, and so forth. The applicability and power of statistical methods is thus much greater for a class model than for the individual claimant model, given the theoretical basis of most statistical methods. When an individual claimant model is used, one point of attack is the definition of the group against which the plaintiff or plaintiffs are to be compared.

Testifying. If any employee or representative of an institution is put in the position of being required to give testimony at a legal proceeding, the following guidelines should be kept in mind:

The Pre-Testimony Conference. Even if the representative of an institution has already testified, he or she should discuss with the attorney in charge the potential questions that may arise, and the nature of his or her testimony in general. This is not intended to be a coaching session, but rather a "what if" session. For the representative who has never testified, this conference should include a run-through of the mechanics of the proceedings.

The Purpose of Testimony. The representative should always remember that the purpose of testimony is to communicate information in a way the audience can understand. If the representative is a researcher or a member of the decision support groups, or he or she should also remember that testifying is not an opportunity for airing personal opinions on matters not specifically related to the case at hand. It is also not the appropriate time to attempt to gain recognition for new or innovative procedures that have been used or developed.

Establishing Credibility. If the representative is testifying as an expert with respect to his or her role in preparing the defense of the institution, one of the most difficult but most important tasks is to establish credibility. For an expert, a vita or resume may be submitted summarizing academic credentials and relevant experience. A copy of this resume may be requested by the plaintiffs prior to the proceedings in which the testimony is to be given; they will have the opportunity to challenge the accuracy and relevance of the witness's credentials.

While academic credentials and relevant experience are very important in establishing credibility, the demeanor, comportment, and attitude of the witness giving testimony can either enhance or lessen credibility. The following points should be kept in mind:

1. The witness should not try to give the appearance of being an expert in too many fields. For example, if a question is asked that is outside a witness's field of expertise, then the witness should not feel uncomfortable stating this fact.

2. If the witness comes from an academic background, he or she should always remember that the presentation is not being made to an academic audience. In particular, he or she should guard against giving the appearance of patronizing the audience.

3. Opinions should be given only when specifically requested and should be labeled as such. Personal opinions and beliefs of a possibly sensitive nature especially should not be volunteered. If the line of testimony gets led away from questions directly related to the case, the judge or one of the attorneys will probably bring this to the attention of the court. If the line of questioning does not get directed back to relevant questions, the witness may ask for an elaboration of the question or an explanation of how the question relates to the case at hand.

Use of Jargon or Technical Terminology. The use of jargon or technical terminology should be avoided, if at all possible. When it is not possible to avoid the use of jargon, an effort should be made to provide a comprehensive definition of each of the terms used. In particular, do not use an excessive amount of jargon or technical terminology in an attempt to establish credibility or impress the judge or jury. Such actions may be perceived as attempts to cover up a lack of knowledge or to direct the audience's attention away from the results of the analyses.

The Audience. As a witness, the researcher or institutional representative should realize that the appropriate audience for a presentation is the judge and jury, not the courtroom audience or the opposing attorney. While the level of the presentation should be targeted at the judge and jury, this can be a particularly difficult task. The witness will probably have no prior knowledge of the ability or knowledge level of the audience and will not have the opportunity to ask questions to determine whether the audience understands the presentation material. It is quite likely that if the judge does not understand a point, he or she will ask for clarification; however, if the presentation is made to a jury, no such clarification may be asked for. In essence, the only clue the researcher may have is the facial expressions or body language of the audience. The witness should pay close attention to any and all clues he or she is given and elaborate if it seems necessary.

Harassment. The opposing attorney may attempt to rattle or unnerve the witness by asking irrelevant questions or by interrupting answers. The witness should not allow the attorney to get the upper hand in such situations and should feel free to finish answering the questions that have been asked. This can be done, for example, by simply responding, "If you will allow me to finish." Also, the institution's attorney should pay attention and should object if such tactics are used.

Depositions and Affidavits. Although an institutional representative may not have to testify at either the class-certification stage or the trial, it is likely that he or she will be required to provide evidence in the form of an affidavit or submit to the taking of a deposition. For a member of the decision support group, for example, this affidavit or deposition might deal with the characteristics and sources of the data that were used for producing any requested reports or responses to interrogatories.

The affidavit is simply a written statement prepared by the representative in response to specific questions that have been raised. The statement is sworn to and notarized and can be submitted as evidence. The deposition is an opportunity for the opposing attorney to question the representative. The questions and answers are taken down and may be submitted as evidence. Note that, in such a situation, the representative will be under oath and subject to the same legal penalties for making false statements that apply to any testimony given in court.

The importance of a pre-deposition briefing by the attorney cannot be underestimated. In such a briefing, the attorney should explain to the representative the types of questions that will probably be asked and the information that will be requested. It is very important that the attorney be fully informed of all pertinent information possessed by the representative.

The deposition process provides the opposing attorney with a chance to gather information that might be used in court to attack the credibility of the representative of the institution, either personally or professionally, or to demonstrate the existence of a bias. In responding to the questions, the representative should answer truthfully but only with sufficient information to satisfy the questions that have been posed; in other words, the representative should not volunteer any information.

The representative may be asked to play another role in the deposition process. It is possible that he or she will be asked to sit in on depositions the institution may take of the plaintiff or the plaintiff's expert, allowing the attorney to consult with the representative while collecting technical information from the other side. The plaintiff will also have this option, and the representative of the institution should not be surprised to find the plaintiff's representative or experts present at the taking of his or her depositions.

Summary

The risk of litigation for institutions is real, and the institution that recognizes this risk and is prepared has gone a long way in limiting the damages that can be incurred in the litigation process. This preparation involves the following steps:
- The recognition and admission that a potential problem exists and the willingness on the part of the administration to squarely face the problem
- An understanding of the statutes under which litigation can be brought and the basic models of proof that can be used to support the claims that are made
- A basic understanding of the litigation process, including the stages and the requirements of each stage
- The identification of a potential team to provide support for the defense of the institution if litigation occurs. (This step is made easier if the institution already has an ongoing internal monitoring system.)

There is simply no way that this chapter can delineate all of the information an institution needs to defend itself. The information provided here is intended only to serve as a starting point. The key to the successful defense of an institution, and in some instances the prevention of litigation, is the team just mentioned and their cumulative skills and knowledge.

Appendix A: "The Plaintiff's Discovery Checklist"

The following checklist was built around "The Plaintiff's Discovery Checklist," published in the *Equal Employment Practice Guide* (1980). The information has been modified slightly to fit this chapter's focus on institutions, and annotation has sometimes been

added to illustrate the points more clearly. The outline is not intended to be complete but only to serve as a solid foundation.
1. Background Information
   a. Ownership/Funding. Is the institution privately funded and run, or are state or federal funds and supervision involved?
   b. Organization Structure. What is the organizational structure of the institution? Does the institution have a governing board in the form of a board of directors, board of regents, and so forth? What is the chain of command at the institution, from the president on down?
   c. Managerial and Supervisory Personnel. Who are the managerial and supervisory personnel? What are their titles, job responsibilities, and so on, and whom do they report to?
   d. Procedures, Policies, Practices. If the claims being made deal with employment, then this would involve personnel procedures, policies, and practices. However, if the claims being made have to do with students, then the procedures, policies and practices would be directed toward admissions, grading, recruitment and the like.
   e. Federal Contractor. Is the institution a federal contractor, or does the institution receive any type of federal aid?
   f. Existence of an Affirmative Action Program: Analysis of Equal Employment Opportunity Profile. Does the institution have an affirmative action program in effect, and if so, what does an analysis of the profile reveal?
   g. Equal Employment Opportunity Reports. Copies of the institution's EE0-6 or EE0-1 reports, depending on which applies.
   h. Existence of Job Descriptions, Admission Requirements, and so forth. Claims involving employment would require copies of any and all job descriptions. Claims involving students would require copies of all admissions requirements and related material.
2. Recruitment Information.
   a. Policies, Practices, Procedures.
   b. Managerial and Supervisory Personnel Responsible for Recruitment. Who are the managerial and supervisory personnel responsible for recruitment? What are their job titles and specific responsibilities?
   c. Sources for Job Applicants or Students. With respect to job applicants, do they come from the immediate geographical area, countywide, statewide, from other institutions? With respect to students, are there certain feeder high schools or other institutions?
   d. Written Directives, Procedures.

e. Training of Recruitment Personnel. Do recruitment personnel receive any special training, and if so, what is the nature and content of that training?
   f. Recruitment Brochures, Pamphlets.
   g. Job Titles or Positions for Recruitment. With respect to personnel, what job titles or positions are being recruited? If the focus is on student recruitment, are students in particular disciplines, or are groups having particular academic credentials or demographic characteristics being recruited?
   h. Race, Sex, and Ethnicity (R/S/E) Statistics for Applicant Flow.
3. Selection and Hire Information
   a. Policies, Practices, Procedures.
   b. Employment-Admissions Selection Process from Initial Contact Through Selection or Rejection. What steps are involved in the hiring-admission selection process, including forms to be completed, aptitude tests, interviews, and so on?
   c. Qualification Requirements, Weight Afforded Each, Changes. What are the basic qualifications for each position filled by a new hire? With respect to students, what are the basic qualifications for admission? Have these requirements changed? What weights are applied to each of the qualifications?
   d. Managerial and Supervisory Persons with Responsibility and Authority for Selection and Hire Procedures, Policies, Practices.
   e. R/S/E Statistics for Applicants for Each Job.
   f. R/S/E Statistics for New Hires for Each Job.
   g. R/S/E Statistics for New Hires with All Desired Qualifications for Each Job.
   h. R/S/E Statistics for New Hires Without All Desired Qualifications for Each Job.
   i. R/S/E Statistics for Average Starting Salary for New Hires for Each Job.
4. Testing Information.
   a. Policies, Practices, Procedures. Are tests required? If tests are required, who administers the tests? when must they be taken? and how are the results used and weighted?
   b. Purpose and Reasons. What is the purpose behind the tests? Are they designed to test for specific job-related skills, general aptitude, academic potential, and so on?
   c. Jobs Tested, Reasons for Change. In the employment situation, which jobs are tested for? Has this changed, and if so, what were the reasons for the change?
   d. Test Validation Studies and Results, Including When and

Who. Have the tests that are being used been validated and if so, when and by whom? What were the results of these validation studies? In the case of employment testing, do studies exist that test the job relatedness of the tests? In an academic setting, do studies exist that explore the relationship between test results and academic success?

   e. R/S/E Statistics for Persons Tested.
5. Assignment Information.
   a. R/S/E Statistics for Initial Assignment into Jobs.
   b. Identify Jobs in Which a Specific Race, Sex, or National Origin Were Excluded by Policy or Practice.
   c. Identify Any Jobs Restricted Due to Federal, State, or Local Law or Regulations.
   d. Written Policies, Practices or Procedures on Assignment.
   e. Managerial or Supervisory Personnel with Assignment Responsibility. What are their names and job titles and to whom do they report?
6. Pay Systems Information.
   a. Description of Each Pay System. When are the employees paid? What compensation is given to employees other than salary? What are the pay rates for each job title and level? Are the employees paid hourly or are they salaried? Are there shift differentials? In general, anything having to do with the payroll system may be requested, including whether or not the system is computerized and the structure and content of the files.
   b. Description of Job Grading Sytem. Are there multiple salary levels for a given job title? Are there shift differentials? How are the levels defined?
   c. Factors in Assigning Salary to Job Title. How are salary levels determined for a given job title and level? For example, for public institutions, are the wage scales set by the state, or by union contract?
   d. Managerial and Supervisory Personnel in Charge of Pay. What are their names and job titles?
   e. Documents Relevant to Pay. These include records such as time sheets, payroll journals, union contracts, and records of overtime payment.
7. Performance Evaluation Information.
   a. Policies, Practices and Procedures for Employee Performance Evaluations. Who is responsible for developing and implementing these policies, practices, and procedures?
   b. Written Instructions, Forms, Documents for Employee Perfor-

mance Evaluations. Who is responsible for constructing and distributing the documents? Which managerial and supervisory personnel have responsibility for constructing and distributing these documents? Who has access to these documents?
c. Validity Studies. Has the validity of these evaluation procedures been studied or, to be more specific, just how valid are the evaluation procedures?
d. Training of Evaluators. What kind of training is given to the individuals conducting the evaluation? Who conducts the training?
e. Job Titles of Employees Evaluated. Are all employees evaluated, or just individuals in certain positions? What are the job titles of the individuals evaluated?
f. Purpose of Evaluation; Appeal Process? Is promotion dependent on the results of the evaluation process? Can an individual be dismissed based on the evaluation results? Is there an appeal process for an employee to contest his evaluation?
g. R/S/E Impact of Performance Evaluation.
8. Promotion Information.
   a. Policies, Practices, Procedures.
   b. Written Directives, Instructions, Documents for Promotion. Who has copies of these documents? When are these documents distributed? Who has the responsibility for the construction and distribution of these documents?
   c. Method by Which Promotees Are Selected—Qualifications and Procedures. How are promotees determined? Is the method known to all employees? Who has the responsibility for determining which individuals are promoted? Is there any mechanism for automatic promotion?
   d. R/S/E Statistics of Persons with Promotional Responsibility or Authority.
   e. R/S/E Statistics of Persons Promoted or Demoted as of Each Relevant Year to Each Relevant Job.
   f. Job Vacancy Postings. How are job vacancies advertised? Are they posted and, if so, who has access to these postings?
   g. Existence of Lines of Progression—Job Chains. Are there traditional or formalized lines of progression? If so, which employees are aware of these lines of progression? How is this information distributed?
   h. Seniority System, Union Contract, Job Titles Applied To. Is there a seniority system or a union contract? What job titles and levels are covered?

i. Trainee Programs for Promotables. Are there training programs? Who has access to these programs? Are these programs formal or informal? How are individuals selected for these programs?
9. Transfer Information.
　　a. Policies, Practices, Procedures.
　　b. Identification of Person(s) in Control. Which managerial and supervisory personnel have the responsibility or authority when it comes to transfers? What is the race, sex, and ethnic breakdown for these individuals?
　　c. Written Documents Relating to Transfer. Who has the responsibility for constructing and maintaining these documents? Who has access to the documents?
　　d. R/S/E Impact of Transfer Procedures.
　　e. Seniority System, Union Contract Job Titles Applicable To. What are the limitations of the transfer policies, procedures, or practices? Are these limited by seniority systems, union contracts, and the like?
10. Training Information.
　　a. Policies, Practices, and Procedures.
　　b. Identification of Person(s) in Control. What managerial and supervisory personnel have the responsibility and authority for training and the selection of individuals for training? What is the race, sex, and ethnic breakdown of these individuals?
　　c. Written Documents Relating to Training. What managerial and supervisory personnel have the responsibility and authority for these documents? Who has access to these documents?
　　d. Purpose of Training, Availability. What is the purpose of the training? For which job titles and levels is training available? Is the training available to all employees?
　　e. R/S/E Impact.
　　f. Promotion Prerequisite for Any Job Titles. Is training a prerequisite for promotion for any job title or level?
11. Benefits Information.
　　a. Policies, Practices, Procedures. Which managerial and supervisory personnel are responsible for determining and administering these?
　　b. Written Documents Describing or Relating to Benefits. Who is responsible for the construction and maintenance of the documents? Who has access to these documents? Are they available to all employees?
　　c. Lists of All Benefits and Bases for Eligibility. What job ben-

efits in addition to salary exist? Who is eligible for these benefits? Do all employees receive the same benefits?
    d. R/S/E Impact on Benefits.
    e. Identification of Person(s) Who Have Control, Responsibility, and Knowledge of Benefits.
12. Maternity Information.
    a. Policies, Practices, Procedures.
    b. Written Documents Describing or Relating to Maternity of Employees. Which managerial and supervisory personnel are responsible for constructing and maintaining these documents? Who has access to these documents?
    c. Identification of Person(s) Who Have Control, Responsibility, or Knowledge of Employment Status of Pregnant Employees.
    d. Identification of Employment Policies, Practices, and Procedures Applicable Only to Pregnant Employees. Who administers these? Have any changes occurred and why have these changes been made?
13. Affirmative Action Information.
    a. Policies, Practices, Procedures.
    b. Written Documents Describing or Relating to Affirmative Action by Defendant. Which managerial and supervisory personnel have responsibility or authority for these documents?
    c. Identification of Person(s) Who Have Control, Responsibility, Knowledge of Company's Affirmative Action Policies, Practices, Procedures.
    d. Reason, Purpose, and Length of Time in Effect of Affirmative Action Plan. If an Affirmative Action Plan is in effect, when was it implemented? who mandated and supervised the plan? who is in charge of seeing that the plan is carried out?

References

Additional Provisions of the Age Discrimination in Employment Act Amendments of 1978, 95 U.S.C., 2d sess., 92 Stat. 189, Public Law 95-256.

Age Discrimination in Employment Act of 1967, 29 U.S.C. Sec. 621, et seq.

Baldus, D. C. and Cole, J. W. L. *Statistical Proof of Discrimination*. New York: McGraw-Hill, 1980.

Becker, G. S. *The Economics of Discrimination*. 2nd Edition. Chicago: University of Chicago Press, 1971.

Bien, D. D. and Santangelo, L. "Some Judicial Uses of Statistical Methods in Title VII Discrimination Cases." *Proceedings of the Social Statistics Section.* Washington, D.C.: American Statistical Association, 1982.

Boulding, I. E. "Toward a Theory of Discrimination" In P. A. Wallace (Ed.), *Equal Employment Opportunity and the AT&T Case*. Cambridge, Mass.: The MIT Press, 1976.
Castaneda v. Partida, 97 S. Ct. 1272, 1280-1282 (1977).
Equal Pay Act of 1963, 29 U.S.C. Sec. 201, et seq., Sec 206 (d).
General Telephone Co. of the Southwest v. Falcon, 457 U.S. 147, 156, (1982).
Hazelwood School District v. United States, 97 S. Ct. 2736, 2741 (1977).
International Brotherhood of Teamsters v. United States, 431 U.S. 324, 336 (1977).
Jones v. Alfred H. Mayer Co., 392 U.S. 409 (1968).
"The Plaintiff's Discovery Checklist." *Equal Employment Practice Guide*. Vol. 2. Washington, D.C.: Federal Bar Association, 1980.
Rehabilitation Act of 1973, 29 U.S.C. Vol. 791.
Strickler, G. M., Jr. *PLI Federal Litigation Practice*. Mineola, N.Y.: Practicing Law Institute, 1979.
Thurow, L. C. *Poverty and Discrimination*. Washington, D.C.: Brookings Institution, 1969.
Tribe, L. H. *American Constitutional Law*. The Foundation Press, 1978.
U.S. Bureau of National Affairs. *The Civil Rights Act of 1964: Text, Analysis, Legislative History*. Operations Manual. Washington, D.C.: Bureau of National Affairs, 1964.

Bernard Yancey, research associate in the Office of the Dean of Students at the University of Texas at Austin, has been an expert witness in a variety of labor litigation cases and has conducted numerous workshops concerning the use of computers and statistics.

The number of regression studies being employed in sex discrimination cases is increasing. The need for caution in the use of multiple regression must be emphasized, however, due to the many assumptions, limitations, and idiosyncrasies associated with this approach.

Statistical Issues and Concerns in Court Cases

*Dennis D. Hengstler,
Gerald W. McLaughlin*

It has often been stated, "there are three types of lies: lies, damn lies, and statistics." Seldom do statistics play a more critical role than in discrimination cases brought before the courts. The statistics are often presented as fact, with the hope of establishing a truth. It is not uncommon, however, for plaintiffs and defendants to arrive at different conclusions based on different statistics derived from the same data source. Quite naturally, a cry is heard that "statistics don't lie, only statisticians do."

The Courts' Reaction to Statistics in Discrimination Cases

Before examining the various methodological and statistical concerns in discrimination cases, it is important to understand the courts' previous approach to university discrimination cases. For many years the courts have been reluctant to get involved in the hiring, promotion, and salary decisions of colleges and universities. As one federal appeals court stated: "Of all fields that the federal courts should hesitate to invade and take over, education and faculty appointments at a university level are probably the least suited for federal court supervision" *(Faro* v. *New York University,* 1974). Recently, the courts have taken an opposing position regarding such cases. In *Sweeney* v. *Board of Trustees of Keene State College* (1978, p. 176), the judge inferred that the courts should not keep a "hands off" policy regarding the salary, promotion, and hiring decisions of a college, "thereby abdicating responsibility entrusted them by Congress, but should provide [a] forum for litigation of complaints of sex discrimination in institutions of higher learning as readily as for other Title VII suits." We can, therefore, expect the courts to be more receptive to salary discrimination suits and to develop a critical eye in evaluating the promotion and salary decision-making processes of academia.

A second judicial concern is the courts' receptiveness to the use of statistics in sex discrimination cases. The Supreme Court recognized in *McDonnell Douglas Corp.* v. *Green* (1973) that the quantum of proof sufficient to constitute a prima facie case cannot be expressed in any general rule and that the factors and statistics used will necessarily vary in Title VII cases. A major concern of the judges, however, is the difficulty in comprehending complicated statistics. As one federal district court judge indicated *(Otero* v. *Mesa Co. Valley School Dist.,* 1979, p. 331): "Judges are quite handicapped in trying to understand this [statistical] testimony. . . . All a trial judge whose statistics course dates back forty-five years can do is try to use his limited knowledge of this quasi-mathematical approach to a problem and then temper the argued for results with a pinch of common sense."

Even with their limited knowledge of statistics, the courts have continued to uphold the use of statistics in discrimination cases. In both the *Hazelwood School District* v. *United States* (1977) and *International Brotherhood of Teamsters* v. *United States* (1977) cases, the Supreme Court ruled that statistics alone may be sufficient to establish a prima facie case of discrimination. The court further stressed in the Teamsters' case: "Statistics are equally competent in proving employment discrimination. We caution only that statistics are not irrefutable; they come in infinite variety and, like any other kind of evidence, they may be rebutted. In short, their usefulness depends on all of the surrounding facts and circumstances."

Statistical Concerns in Salary Equity Studies

The remaining discussion will focus on statistical concerns in sex discrimination cases, although the concerns are shared equally in race and age discrimination cases. In conducting salary equity studies, almost all the models or approaches used are variations of the descriptive, paired-comparison, or regression analysis approach. Numerous books and articles have discussed the limitations and appropriateness of these statistical and evaluative models for analyzing salary equity between the sexes (Baldus and Cole, 1975, 1980; Finkelstein, 1980; Fisher, 1980; Gray and Scott, 1980; Hengstler and others, 1982; Koch and Chizmar, 1976; Nevill, 1975; Pezzullo and Brittingham, 1979; Reagan and Maynard, 1974; Scott, 1977; and Simpson and Rosenthal, 1982). A brief summary of the major strengths and weaknesses of the different approaches is presented here.

Descriptive Method. As indicated in earlier chapters, the first step in establishing the prima facie case of discrimination is to show that a sizable difference exists between the salaries and ranks of the minority class and the rest of the faculty. In the early discrimination cases before the courts, plaintiffs relied almost exclusively on the descriptive method for establishing a prima facie case of discrimination. The success of those plaintiffs set a precedent for subsequent plaintiffs to use this particular approach (for example, *Albemarle Paper Co. v. Moody*, 1975; *McDonnell Douglas Corp. v. Green*, 1973).

One of the reasons this method can be effective in establishing the prima facie case is that direct evidence of discrimination is seldom available. Thus, circumstantial statistical evidence, often aggregated data in the form of frequencies and percentages, can be accepted as evidence of discrimination. As interpreted in *Griggs v. Duke Power Company* (1971), the mere demonstration of a percentage difference, without an explanation in terms of differing job-related abilities, is sufficient to constitute a violation of Title VII. If the plaintiffs go on to present statistically significant testing data (for example, Chi-square, analysis of variance, t-test) to demonstrate that salary differences could not have occurred by chance, an even more compelling case can be made.

Although frequencies and percentages can be effective in establishing a prima facie case of discrimination, they can often be refuted by simple demographic analyses. Invalid assumptions are often made when data is aggregated. Within the context of higher education, such analyses could include a breakdown of the salaries by rank, highest degree, tenure, discipline, different samples or cohorts, and so on. (Most institutional research offices are capable of conducting this type of analysis for the university.) In *Keys* v. *Lenoir Rhyne College* (1977), the court ruled that the plaintiff failed to establish a prima facie case, even though evidence revealed that the average male faculty salary was higher than that of the average female. The court reasoned that there was no salary differential when teaching positions were analyzed, and that the plaintiff made no comparison of salaries by discipline or department.

Simpson and Rosenthal (1982) have pointed out the various limitations and assumptions of the descriptive method in discrimination studies and the ways to refute such studies. Many of the descriptive studies fail to take into account: first, the historical trend of women gravitating to certain disciplines that are lower paying due to lower demand and lower economic market value; second, the larger number of women in the lower ranks due in part to the effects of affirmative action legislation in increasing the number of entry level positions for women; third, the relationships between academic rank and salary; and fourth, the qualifications and criteria for promotion, where women tend to remain in certain ranks longer due to their lack of a terminal degree in their respective disciplines (Bikel and others, 1975).

Paired-Comparison Method. The second method for determining possible sex discrimination in faculty salaries is the paired-comparison method, also referred to as the matching, counterparting, or counterfactual approach. In essence, the paired-comparison method attempts to match a male counterpart to each female faculty member. Any discrepancies between male and female salaries are assumed to be the result of sex discrimination, thereby establishing the plaintiff's prima facie case of discrimination.

One obvious major problem confronting the paired-comparison approach is the identification of appropriate pairs. In a study on the status of men and women at the University of Chicago *(Women in the University of Chicago,* 1970), department chairpersons were asked to select for each female faculty member in their department the man most nearly matching her in qualifications and responsibilities. Only 68 percent of all faculty women could be matched.

The problem of matching is further complicated in departments such as nursing and home economics, where there may be an insufficient number of male faculty colleagues with whom meaningful salary comparisons can be made. In situations where no satisfactory pairs can be identified, the female faculty member's salary should be compared with the average salary of males within the department with comparable qualifications or the salary offered to a recruit with similar qualifications. A comparison of the department's salary structure with other departments on campus or similar departments at other institutions may also be helpful.

There are other disadvantages to the matching approach aside from the problem of identifying appropriate pairs, especially if it is the plaintiff who selects her counterpart. First, the plaintiff often lacks the knowledge and objectivity that a chairperson or dean has in regard to the qualifications, experience, and responsibilities of her subordinates. A defendant might, with little effort, successfully challenge all of the plaintiff's matches, as in the case of *Faro* v. *New York University* (1974). On the other hand, if the plaintiff asked the defendant to select the matches, the results might reflect the defendant's bias (Greenfield, 1977). A second problem is the atmosphere of tension created when counterparts must be identified. As Prather and Smith (1974, p. 3) state: "The emotional upheaval resulting from the ramifications of having to identify and agree on matching counterparts is an obvious drawback that could result in a negative climate for all parties. It also provides no operational basis for keeping salaries in balance after parity has been reached." A final disadvantage to the paired-comparison method is the fact that it can only demonstrate whether inequity exists; it cannot determine the extent of inequity (Pezzullo and Brittingham, 1979). The reason the approach cannot determine the extent of inequity is that it does not allow for every possible comparison. There may be several male counterparts with similar qualifications, but the female faculty member or the department chairperson is asked to select only one.

The advantage of the paired-comparison method lies in its simplicity and straightforwardness. It can be easily understood by all, especially by the courts. If the plaintiff is involved in the selection of appropriate pairs or in the salary review process, there may be fewer ill-feelings and less chance of recrimination. This latter point, however, is open to debate (Nevill, 1975).

Regression Analysis Approach. Perhaps the most widely used model in analyzing sex discrimination in faculty salaries is the multiple regression approach. This technique has been employed with varying degrees of success in several sex discrimination cases presented before the courts *(Mecklenburg* v. *Montana Board of Regents of Higher Education,* 1976; *Presseisen* v. *Swarthmore College,* 1978;

Board of Regents of University of Nebraska v. *Dawes,* 1976; *Trout* v. *Hidalgo,* 1981; and *Wilkins* v. *University of Houston,* 1981). One court has recognized the utility of multiple regression by stating: "If properly used, multiple regression analysis is a relatively reliable and accurate method of gauging classwide discrimination" *(Wilkins* v. *University of Houston,* 1981, p. 22007).

Multiple Regression Statistics

Multiple regression is a statistical technique that measures the relationship between a criterion, in this case salary, and a set of predictors (independent variables) presumed to have a direct relationship to the criterion. A major advantage of this approach is that it can determine not only whetther a particular predictor (for example, sex) influenced the criterion (for example, salary) but also how much the predictor influenced the criterion; that is, it assigns a number (called a beta or regression weight) approximating how much the value of a given predictor should be weighted in the formula estimating the actual salary of an individual. (For a complete discussion of multiple regression, the reader is referred to Cohen and Cohen, 1975, or Kerlinger and Pedhazur, 1973.)

To interpret the results of the regression analysis, one needs to understand various statistics produced by the regression method. The first is the standard error of the regression weight, which provides a measure of the weight's reliability. The larger the standard error, the less accurate the weight is in estimating the true effect of a given variable. The significance level of the regression weight is used to determine whether the weight is significantly different from zero or not. This is often tested by the t-statistic. There are numerous factors (for example, size of sample) that can affect the standard error of the regression weight. In turn, the instability of the regression (beta) weights can dramatically affect the prediction of salaries.

The second statistic is the standard error of estimate, which provides an indication of accuracy in predicting a person's salary. In large samples, the chances are ninety-nine out of one hundred that the predicted salary lies within two and one-half standard errors of estimate. The larger the standard error of estimate, the less accurate the prediction of the person's salary.

The final statistic that is necessary in interpreting the results of multiple regression analysis is the multiple correlation *(R)* and R^2. The multiple R denotes the correlation between the criterion and the optimally weighted combination of predictors. By squaring the multiple R, one obtains a measure of the amount of variance in the criterion that is accounted for in the set of predictors in the regression equation. An important feature of R^2 is that it indicates the amount of additional variance accounted for in the criterion by a given predictor, when that predictor is first excluded and then included in the regression equation. The difference between the two obtained R^2s will indicate the amount of additional variance in the criterion (salary) that is accounted for by the predictor (sex). The regression weight for sex may be significantly different from zero, yet sex may account for only a very small percentage of the variance in salaries. This was one of the reasons given by the court in ruling against the plaintiff's charge of sex discrimination in *Wilkins* v. *University of Houston* (1981).

Limitations of Multiple Regression Approach

To fully understand the regression model, one must be aware of the assumptions, limitations, and specific characteristics of the model. The following discussion will deal with only a few of these characteristics, since a more detailed treatment is beyond the scope of this chapter. For such a discussion, one should consult: Baldus and Cole, 1980; Fisher, 1980; Greenfield, 1977; Muffo and Hengstler, 1983; Pezzullo and Brittingham, 1979; and Rosenthal and others, 1981. Two characteristics that seem to affect the results of a multiple regression study most are the type of predictors and the type of sample employed.

Predictors. In estimating salaries in the higher-education setting, numerous predictors can be utilized: sex, academic rank, discipline or departmental affiliation, number of years in rank, highest degree, terminal degree, number of years employed at the institution, prior experience, age, tenure status, administrative responsibility, graduate faculty, books and articles published, grants, honors, offices held, student ratings of instruction, and peer ratings.

There are several problems inherent in selecting a set of predictors. The first is the actual number of predictors that one should use. As the number of predictors approaches the sample size, the power of the test decreases, possibly resulting in a spuriously high correlation. As Cohen and Cohen state (1975, p. 160): "Having more variables [predictors] when fewer are possible, increases the risks of both finding things that are not and failing to find things that are." Including an exceedingly high number of predictors might result in the elimination of sex as a predictor in the regression equation, when it should have been included.

The second problem in the selection of predictors is that of multicollinearity. Multicollinearity refers to the substantial correlation between some or all of the predictors, which can lead to misinterpretations of the results. Assume, for instance, that sex is correlated with salary as well as with number of years of experience and highest degree. Depending on the order of presentation, sex might enter as a significant predictor of salary even in the absence of sex discrimination. The reason is that sex would be serving as a proxy variable for number of years of experience and highest degree. In other words, the true variance in salary accounted for by number of years of experience and highest degree is being explained by sex due to the strong relationship (correlation) between the three predictors. Thus, multicollinearity serves to mask the true relationship between the predictors and the criterion.

Birnbaum (1979) discusses the problem of collinearity using an example with three variables; merit (M), salary $(\$)$, and sex (X) and fairness in allocating salaries. If all three of these variables are a function of some underlying variable, say quality (Q) then

(1)
$$\beta Z(\$) = q\$(Q) + si$$
$$\beta Z(M) = qm(M) + mi$$
$$\beta Z(X) = qx(Q) + xi$$

where the Z represents standard scores.

The partial regression of salary on sex in the presence of quality is

(2)
$$\beta(\$)X.M = \frac{q\$qx\,(1 - qm^2)}{1 - (qxqm)^2}$$

The collinearity of sex and merit is $rxm = qxqm$.

It is obvious that unless qm is zero (for example, merit is not related to quality minus an unexpected event), then collinearity occurs unless $qx = 0$. If $qx = 0$, the regression in (2) goes to zero. If there is collinearity, then (2) goes to zero only if either $qm = 1$ (for example, merit is perfectly related to quality) or $r_{\$x} = r_{\$m}r_{xm}$.

While it does not remove the problem, use of a two-step procedure (McLaughlin and others, 1983) reduces the size of the error made in statistically estimating discrimination from a regression model. The two-step procedure first estimates the salary from the measure or measures of merit. The unexplained part of the salary is then regressed on sex. In terms of the variables used above, the regression of the residual on sex yields a weight of

(3) $$\beta(\$ - \hat{\$})x = q\$qx(1 - qm^2).$$

This shows that the two-step procedure yields an estimate that is more nearly zero, the appropriate value under the fairness model just shown. Conceptually, this procedure defines discrimination as the variation in salary that can be explained only by sex. It also has the advantage of simplicity. As can be shown, if the salary is predicted by merit, then the weight in (3) is the sum of the mean residuals of the males minus the mean residuals of the females. For example, if the male mean residual is $758 and the female mean residual is -$1,516 then the difference in salaries uniquely explained by sex is $2,274. The significance of discrimination under this interpretation can be determined by a simple t-test for independent means.

Several other observations can be made concerning the relationship for either (2) or (3). In both cases the size of the perceived bias is inversely proportional to qm. If qm goes to one, the regression weight goes to zero. One way to increase qm is to increase the reliability of the measure of merit. Second, anything that reduced the correlation of merit and salary will inflate the bias. This causes concern with the use of Scott's (1979) best male model if the females have a distribution of merit different from males. Use of males only restricts the range on all three variables and tends to give lower correlation of merit with salary. The equations also suggest that knowledge of the reliability of the merit variable (qm^2) could be used to estimate the amount of inflation in the statistical estimation of bias.

The third problem associated with the selection of predictors is the inclusion of inappropriate variables in the equation, or conversely, the failure to take important variables into account. An example of the former can be found in *Stastny* v. *Southern Bell Telephone & Telegraph Co.* (1978), where the court observed that the defendant's regressions incorporated predictors (in this case, marital status) that were "tainted." An example of the consequences of failing to include what the court considers an important predictor can be found in *Wilkins* v. *University of Houston* (1981), where the plaintiff's lack of a market or academic discipline factor in the analysis was a major reason the court ruled against her.

A final problem associated with the selection of predictors is the inclusion of academic rank in the regression equation. Since rank is generally highly correlated with salary, the inclusion of rank will substantially increase the amount of variance in salary being explained but may at the same time conceal the influence of sex discrimination. As has been shown (Braskamp and others, 1978), the existence of salary discrimination tends to coincide with discrimination in the awarding of rank, so that both academic rank and salary are integral parts of the same reward structure. Using one measure of reward to predict another only confuses the analysis.

The courts' reaction to the use of rank in regression analyses has varied. In *Mecklenburg v. Montana Board of Regents of Higher Education* (1976) the court objected to the defendant's regression analysis, since the regressions were conducted within rank, and the court had previously found discrimination against women in the promotion and tenure process. In contrast, the court in *Presseisen v. Swarthmore College* (1978) found the plaintiff's regression analysis unacceptable because rank was not included; the court had previously ruled that the plaintiff's claim of discrimination in promotions had not been sustained.

Should rank be included in the regression equations? It would appear that the courts are beginning to say yes, under special circumstances. As summarized by Finkelstein (1980, p. 742), the courts generally agree that "in the normal case, rank should be included as an explanatory variable only when there is clear evidence of neutral and objective standards that have consistently been followed in granting rank, so that there is no chance for discrimination. Most academic institutions have not yet developed such standards, although it may be possible to do so."

Samples. The second important characteristic, after consideration of predictors, that affects regression equations is the selection of the sample. Different types of samples can be employed in a regression analysis. The American Association of University Professors Salary Kit (Scott, 1977) recommends running the regression equation on a homogeneous group (department or discipline) of male faculty members and then applying the obtained regression weights to the female faculty data, in order to arrive at predicted salaries. The predicted salaries of male and female salaries should then be compared for potential sex discrimination. The econometric approach to studying salary equity (Ferber and Kordick, 1978; Hoffman, 1976; Johnson and Stafford, 1974; and Katz, 1973) often uses the entire university sample with sex as a predictor.

If university data bases are employed, having an adequate number of female faculty memebers in the sample should not generally be a problem. However, if the sample is restricted to department or discipline data bases, there may be only one or two females included in the sample. If the number of males in the sample is fairly large, the true effect of sex on salary may be masked by the restricted number of females in the sample. Although logically, it would be desirable to conduct such analyses within individual departments or like disciplines, at most institutions, the sample sizes involved would be so small that concerns about the validity of the results might be raised.

Dividing the university population into smaller homogeneous segments creates an additonal problem. That is, as the population size decreases, the disparity must be increasingly large to be statistically significant. The defendants in *Trout v. Hidalgo* (1981) used this approach to try to prove that sex was not a significant predictor in the smaller segmented samples. The court rejected the defendant's methodology and expressed its support in aggregating the samples: "The court does not agree with the view that an aggregation across job lines necessarily destroys the probative value of regressions. Indeed, . . . the technique is superior to methods that entail a fragmentation into populations so small that statistical analysis loses much of its power to find any discrimination" (p. 83).

This situation is analagous to another problem often associated with regression analysis—the restriction of range problem. As Linn (1983) points out, a common problem in testing is that prediction equations are sometimes derived from data on high-ability and homogeneous groups, and then applied to predict the success rates for lower-ability and more heterogeneous groups. The result can be either overprediction or underprediction. If, in a particular instance, male and female faculty members differ significantly with respect to ability or homogeneity, this difference could cause shifts in the prediction equations employed in studying possible sex discrimination.

Other Multiple Regression Issues. The final set of problems to be discussed is associated with the assumptions of the multiple regression approach. Two basic assumptions are those of constant variance and continuous variables (McCullagh and Nelder, 1983). The assumption of constant variance refers to the variance of the criterion variable. If the variance of the predictor variables is not constant, this can be handled by using a weighted least squares approach. Another assumption often associated with multiple regression is that the error terms are normally distributed. It is doubtful, however, that if the distributions are nearly normal and the variance nearly constant, the conclusions drawn from the analyses will be drastically changed (Daniel and Wood, 1980). When employment data at institutions of higher education are being considered, it is more likely that the assumption of continuous predictor and criterion variables will not be met. For example, many data thought to be related to faculty salaries are sometimes nominal in nature (for example, departmental affiliation) or at best an ordered category (for example, rank).

Log-Linear Models. Log-linear models are particularly useful in the situation just noted. There are two main uses of this technique; testing for association of variables and developing logit equations. Testing for association represents an extension of the Chi-square test of independence for two categorical variables, while logit analysis is similar to multiple regression using the folded log of the probability of occurrence as the dependent variable.

The test of association is well established in the two-variable situation. Chi-square analysis allows one to answer the question: Is the decision of tenure independent of gender? The problem arises when considering the year of the decision, and we must ask if the decision of tenure was independent of gender given that particular year of the decision. Log-linear analysis allows the investigation of this more complicated type of question. The frequencies in the cells are reformulated into a log-linear model that can have a term of each main effect and the interaction of the main effects (Payne, 1977).

If all of the main effects and interactions are used in a model, then the estimate of the expected frequencies are equal to the observed frequencies, and the model is called the saturated model. Therefore, a saturated model does not allow one to check for model inadequacy. As terms are removed from the model, there is a difference between the observed frequencies in the data and the frequencies estimated from the model. This difference can then be compared to what might be expected under a null hypotheses of chance. When the difference caused by removing a term becomes too large to have been expected by chance, the conclusion can be reached that the term removed was significantly important in explaining the data.

There are procedures to adjust for empty cells so that the technique does not have the limitation of the traditional Chi-square. It is similar to the ANOVA in that there is a problem when collinearities exist among the independent variables. The extent of this problem can be determined by considering both sequential and marginal type results similar to those provided in ANOVA when unbalanced designs are encountered (for example, SAS Type 1 and Type 4 errors).

In most hypothesis testing using log-linear analyses, a hierarchical procedure is used. In a hierarchical model all main effects and interactions contained in the highest-order interaction in the model are also separately contained in the model. For example, if the interaction of year-sex-decision (YSD) is contained in a model, then the three interactions of year-sex (YS); year-decision (YD); and sex-decision (SD) are included along with the three main effects.

As might be anticipated from these comments, using log-linear analysis requires developing a null model (free from bias), defining a term or terms that represent bias, and determining statistically if the bias term significantly improves the explanation of the observed data. As a starting point, consider the following decision rules for this process:
(1) The interaction of sex with the decision variable (SD) represents potential bias. The same is true of any interaction where this interaction is a component (SDY).
(2) All other terms are free from bias and are included in the null model (S, D, Y, SY). These terms are not considered separately.
(3) The model from (2) is tested against the saturated model to determine if the interaction terms containing bias are statistically significant in explaining observed frequencies.
(4) If (3) shows that there is a statistical indication of bias, terms are added to the null in order of the amount they reduce the poorness of fit. This addition of terms is done in a hierarchical process so that the Chi-squares are additive from model to model.

The process is fairly mechanical up to rule 3. At that point, if one goes to rule 4, the process becomes similar to exploring ANOVA situations. It is less structured and is dependent on a rational strategy of investigation.

Logit analysis is the procedure of developing log-linear models for asymmetric relationships to explain a dichotomous dependent variable. This is comparable to the log-linear procedure just mentioned, when all marginal frequencies with respect to the dependent variable are considered fixed. Here, the approach is similar to the linear regression procedure in that a set of independent variables, along with their interactions, is assumed to influence the dependent variable. The dependent variable is the log of the probability of occurrence divided by one minus the probability of occurrence (that is, the folded log). In the testing of sex bias, the decision variable would be the dependent measure, and the hypotheses being tested would involve determining if the addition of sex and its interactions with other measures made a significant contribution to the explanation of the decision. While this model has not yet been extended, one application of the logit concept would be to consider the implications of using a two-step procedure as recommended in the section on regression.

The use of logit analysis is not yet established in the literature on sex bias. Some papers exist, but the interested reader would best be served by reading Kennedy (1983) and Payne (1977). The standard analysis programs of BMD-P, SPSSX, and SAS have computational programs for the analysis (Hinkle and McLaughlin, in press). While the mathematical model violates the criterion of simplicity, the results of its use can and should be translated back into expected frequencies. The statement can then be made: Considering these factors that are not related to sex bias, we expect x males and y females to receive tenure. These numbers [are, are not] significantly different from what could have occurred by chance.

Salary Adjustment. Adjustment of salaries is the logical step after the analysis of sex bias. The adjustment depends on the method used in the analysis and on the results of the analysis. Birnbaum (1983) suggests that the amount of money for the adjustment is typically less than needed to remove inequities. His conclusion is that the method seen as most fair by the faculty is to adjust salaries based on the relative deficit of the various individuals. This procedure adds together the total deficits of those who are underpaid and divides this sum into the amount set aside for adjusting salaries. This fraction is then multiplied by each individual's deficit to determine the amount of adjustment.

If the analysis used does not show a significant class bias, it may still reveal individuals with salaries substantially below the anticipated salary. If there seems to be no logical reason for the difference, it is good practice to make the appropriate adjustment. In this type of consideration, consider both males and females and also consider both very high positive as well as very negative residuals. Discrepancies are placed into perspective, and the pay schedule can be discussed. Through the pay schedule one can raise valid questions such as, What rewards do we offer at our institution, and are these rewards appropriate?

The question of what a significant class bias is can be answered statistically by the error variance for the model used in the analysis. If the linear regression approach is used, consider using the hyperbolic confidence limits as discussed by Draper and Smith (1981). These confidence limits suggest that our estimates are less reliable as we move away from the average characteristics of the group. Errors made in estimating the regression weights cause this increase in error.

Other assumptions that may come into play in a regression analysis are the independence of the error term and the normal distribution of the error term. The reader is referred to Fisher (1980) for a more elaborate discussion of the issues.

Reverse Regression. A technique that is receiving increasing attention is reverse regression. Again using the earlier notation, where merit *(M)* is regressed on sex *(X)* in the presence of salary.

$$(4) \qquad \beta mx.\$ = \frac{qmqx(1 - q\$^2)}{1(- q\$qx)^2}$$

By analogy, a two-stage procedure for reverse regression produces

$$(5) \qquad \beta(m-\hat{m})X = qmqx(1 - q\$^2).$$

As Birnbaum notes, "The worse the measurement of merit in a study, if one assumes no discrimination, the greater the apparent discrimination when measured by multiple regression" (1979, p. 126). If the equity model is appropriate, then the regression weights in (2) through (5) should have the same sign as the simple correlation of the other independent variables with sex.

The value of reverse regression is still a matter of great debate. See the *Journal of Business and Economic Statistics* (1984) for a range of articles on the topic of reverse regression.

Conclusion

It would appear that the multiple regression technique is the most effective method for analyzing sex discrimination in faculty salaries. The courts are beginning to recognize the utility of this approach, although they harbor some concern over the difficulty in understanding such statistics. The number of regression studies being employed in sex discrimination cases is increasing. The need for caution in the use of multiple regresison must be emphasized, however, due to the many assumptions, limitations, and idiosyncrasies associated with this approach.

References

Albemarle Paper Co. v. Moody, 95 S.Ct. 2362, 2375 (1975).
Baldus, D. C., and Cole, J. W. L. "Beyond the *Prima Facie* Case in Employment Discrimination Law: Statistical Proof and Rebuttal." *Harvard Law Review*, 1975, *89*, 2.
Baldus, D. C., and Cole, J. W. L. *Statistical Proof of Discrimination*. New York: McGraw-Hill, 1980.
Bickel, P. J., Hammel, E. A., and O'Connel, J. W. "Sex Bias in Graduate Admissions: Data from Berkeley." *Science*, 1975, *187*, 398-404.
Birnbaum, M. H. "Procedures for the Detection and Correction of Salary Inequities." In T. R. Pezzullo and B. E. Brittingham (Eds.), *Salary Equity*. Lexington, Mass.: Lexington Books, 1979.
Birnbaum, M. H. "Perceived Equity of Salary Policies." *Journal of Applied Psychology*, 1983, *68* (1), 49-59.
Board of Regents of the University of Nebraska v. Dawes, 522 F.2d 380 (8th Cir. 1975), cert. denied 424 U.S. 914 (1976).
Braskamp, L.A., Muffo, J. A., and Langston, I. W., III. "Determining Salary Equity: Politics, Procedures, and Problems." *Journal of Higher Education*, 1978, *49*, 231-246.
Cohen, J., and Cohen, P. *Applied Multiple Regression-Correlation Analysis for the Behavioral Sciences*. Hillsdale, N.J.: Lawrence Erlbaum, 1975.
Daniel, C., and Wood, F. S. *Fitting Equations to Data*. New York: Wiley, 1980.
Draper, N., and Smith, H. *Applied Regression Analysis*. 2nd ed. New York: Wiley, 1981.
Faro v. New York University, 502 F.2d 1229 (1974).
Ferber, M. A., and Kordick, B. "Sex Differentials in the Earnings of Ph.D.s." *Industrial and Labor Relations Review*, 1978, *31*, 227-238.
Finkelstein, M. O. "The Judicial Reception of Multiple Regression Studies in Race and Sex Discrimination Cases." *Columbia Law Review*, 1980, 737-754.
Fisher, F. "Multiple Regression in Legal Proceedings." *Columbia Law Review*, 1980, *80*, 702-736.
Gray, M. W., and Scott, E. L. "A Statistical Remedy for Statistically Identified Discrimination." *Academe*, 1980, *66*, 174-181.
Greenfield, E. "From Equal to Equivalent Pay: Salary Discrimination in Academia." *Journal of Law and Education*, 1977, *6*, 41-62.
Griggs v. Duke Power Co. 401 U.S. 424, 426, 432 (1971).
Hazelwood School District v. United States, 433 U.S. 399, 97 S.Ct. 2736, 53 L.Ed.2d 768 (1977).
Hengstler, D. D., Muffo, J. A., and Hengstler, G. A. "Salary Equity Studies: The State of the Art." Paper presented at the Association for the Study of Higher Education annual meeting, Washington, D.C., March 1982.
Hinkle, D. E., and McLaughlin, G. W. "Selection of Models in Contingency Tables: A Re-examination." *Research in Higher Education*, in press.
Hoffmann, E. P. "Faculty Salaries: Is There Discrimination by Sex, Race, and Discipline? Additional Evidence." *American Economic Review*, 1976, *66*, 196-198.
International Brotherhood of Teamsters v. United States, 431 U.S. 324, 339, 97 S.Ct. 1843, 1856, 52 L.Ed.2d 396 (1977).
Johnson, G. E., and Stafford, F. P. "The Earnings and Promotion of Women Faculty." *American Economic Review*, 1974, *64*, 888-903.

Journal of Business and Economic Statistics, 1984, *2* (2).
Katz, D. A. "Faculty Salaries, Promotions, and Productivity at a Large University." *American Economic Review*, 1973, *63*, 460-477.
Kennedy, J. J. *Analyzing Qualitative Data: Introductory Log-Linear Analyses for Behavioral Research.* New York: Praeger, 1983.
Kerlinger, F. N., and Pedhazur, E. J. *Multiple Regression in Behavioral Research.* New York: Holt, Rinehart and Winston, 1973.
Keys v. Lenoir Rhyne College, 552 F.2d 579 (1977).
Koch, J. V., and Chizmar, J. F., Jr. "Sex Discrimination and Affirmative Action in Faculty Salaries." *Economic Inquiry*, 1976, *14*, 16-24.
Linn, R. L. P. "Selection Formulas: Implications for Studies of Predictive Bias and Estimations of Educational Effects in Selected Samples." *Journal of Educational Measurement*, 1983, *20*, 1-15.
McCullagh, P., and Nelder, J. A. *Generalized Linear Models.* New York: Chapman and Hall, 1983.
McDonnell Douglas Corp. v. Green, 411 U.S. 974 (1973).
McLaughlin, G. W., Zirkes, M. B., and Mahan, B. T. "Multicollinearity and Testing Questions of Sex Equity." *Research in Higher Education*, 1983, *19* (3), 277-284.
Mecklenburg v. Montana Board of Regents of Higher Education, 93 Empl. Prac. Dec. 11, 438 (D. Mont. 1976).
Muffo, J. A., and Hengstler, D. D. "Statistical Issues in Comparing Women and Men Faculty: Applications in Sex Discrimination." *Journal of Educational Equity and Leadership*, 1983, *3*, 317-326.
Nevill, D. D. "Achieving Salary Equity." *Educational Record*, 1975, *56*, 266-270.
Otero v. Mesa County Valley School District, F.Supp. 326, 331 (D. Colo. 1979).
Payne, C. "Model Fitting." In C. A. O'Muircheartaigh and C. Payne (Eds.), *The Analysis of Survey Data.* Vol. 2. New York: Wiley, 1977.
Pezzullo, T. R., and Brittingham, B. E. (Eds.). *Salary Equity: Detecting Sex Bias in Salaries Among College and University Professors.* Lexington, Mass.: Lexington Books, 1979.
Prather, J. E., and Smith, G. "Salary Prediction Technique—A Tool for Affirmative Action." Paper presented at the Association for Institutional Research Annual Forum, Washington, D.C., May 17, 1974.
Presseisen v. Swarthmore College, 442 F.Supp.. 593 (E.D. Oa. 1977), aff'd. 582 F.2d 1275 (3rd Cir. 1978).
Reagan, B. B., and Maynard, B. J. "Sex Discrimination in Universities: An Approach Through Internal Labor Market Analysis." *AAUP Bulletin*, 1974, *60*, 13-21.
Rosenthal, W. H., Simpson, W. A., and Sperber, W. E. "Using Regression Analysis to Capture Policy in a Sex Discrimination Suit." Paper presented at the Association for Institutional Research Forum, Minneapolis, Minn., May 10, 1981.
Scott, E. L. *Higher Education Salary Evaluation Kit.* Washington, D. C.: American Association of University Professors, 1977.
Scott, E. L. "Linear Models and the Law: Uses and Misuses in Affirmative Action." In *Proceedings of the Social Statistics Section.* Washington, D. C.: American Statistical Association, 1979.
Simpson, W. A., and Rosenthal, W. H. "The Role of the Institutional Researcher in a Sex Discrimination Suit." *Research in Higher Education*, 1982, *16* (1), 3-26.
Stastny v. Southern Bell Telephone & Telegraph Co., 9458 F.Supp. 314 (W.D.N.C. 1978).
Sweeney v. Board of Trustees of Keene State College, 569 F.2d 169 (1978).

Trout v. *Hidalgo,* 517 F.Supp. 873 (1981).
Wilkins v. *University of Houston,* 26 EPD 32101 (5th Cir. 1981).
Women in the University of Chicago. Report of the Committee on University Women, Chicago, Ill., 1970.

Dennis D. Hengstler is director of the Office of Planning and Policy Analysis at the University of Houston, University Park. He is currently involved in budgetary and fiscal studies.

Gerald W. McLaughlin is associate director of institutional research and planning analysis at Virginia Polytechnic Institute and State University. He has done extensive work in applied statistics and in the implications of analytical results. He has served as president of the Southern Association for Institutional Research and is currently editor of the AIR Professional File.

The underrepresentation of blacks in higher education in the state must be remedied by increasing the pool of potential colleagues, not by shifting hiring patterns.

Changing Conditions, Changing Responses: A Case Study of Minority Participation in Indiana Higher Education

John A. Muffo

Background

The study of minority student participation in Indiana began in response to a letter from the Indiana Black Legislative Caucus to the Commissioner of Higher Education in February 1984. In this letter the black caucus, consisting of eight state senators and representatives, asked the commission to work with the presidents of the institutions of higher educatioin to examine the utilization of black faculty and staff. The letter also requested a study of the opportunities for black students to enroll in academic programs that are in high demand.

The letter from the black caucus was the result of several forces operating in the state and the nation at the time. At the state level, a group of black faculty and staff at state universities had come together to form a group to discuss mutual concerns. This group, called the Indiana Coalition of Blacks in Higher Education, found that blacks were underrepresented at each campus, considering the proportion of blacks in the state's population. There seemed to be a feeling among the faculty and staff that blacks were few in number and were kept outside of the academic-social-cultural mainstream at each of their campuses.

At the same time that black faculty and staff were coming together at the state level, the Jesse Jackson for President campaign was taking place on the national level. The earlier decline in the economy seemed to have had a particularly hard impact on racial minorities. There were fewer jobs available, and those that were available either paid poorly or had training requirements that were impossible for most blacks. The Jackson campaign brought out some of the frustrations of those who felt they were losing ground economically and that nobody seemed to care. While the black faculty and staff were not affected by the economic changes as much as others in the black community, the frustration with "business as usual" at their own institutions seems to have become focused at this time.

Interim Report

Overview. The response of the Commission for Higher Education to the black caucus letter was to propose a study limited to the issue of minority student participation in higher education in Indiana. The statutory authority of the commission does not allow it to enter into institutional management, since that is a responsibility limited to the college and university trustees, so that hiring and promotion practices are not within the purview of the commission. In addition, an examination of the data reveals that there is a proportionately low number of blacks on the national level who are eligible to become faculty members and administrators in institutions of higher education.

The *Profile of 1982–83 Recipients of Doctorates* (1983), published by the National Research Council, found blacks receiving only 1,000 out of 31,190 doctorates awarded nationally during that period. Of the 1,000 awarded, 794 were in either education, social sciences, or the arts and humanities; fields where faculty hiring had been very restricted in recent years. This left over 3,000 institutions of higher education, along with the governmental and corporate sectors, to compete nationally for little more than 200 blacks receiving doctorates in high-demand fields. Although the few blacks who are employed at state colleges and universities may have legitimate individual grievances, the solution to the larger problem of black underrepresentation in higher education in the state must lie more in increasing the pool of potential colleagues than in shifting hiring patterns.

The Indiana Commission for Higher Education therefore agreed to conduct a study of minority student participation in higher education. Data sources to be used included those already available to the commission through its coordinating responsibilities within the state, as well as external data sources such as those of the U.S. Bureau of the Census, the state's Department of Public Instruction, and other state coordinating commissions. An advisory group was formed, composed of representatives of the public and independent institutions as well as the state's Department of Public Instruction, to provide advice and counsel to commission staff members conducting the study.

The aim of the advisory group was not so much to solicit the opinions of blacks and other minorities as to tap institutional expertise. The solicitation of opinions and suggestions was to come later. During the early part of the study, when the *Interim Report* was being written, the advisory group was particularly helpful in the analysis of existing data, the development of new data, and the interpretation of the data. Its cooperation also ensured that the credibility of the data would not be called into question, thereby bogging the study down in data questions and undermining its effectiveness.

The *Interim Report on Minority Student Participation* (1984) was the first step in responding to the request of the black caucus. It was designed to be a data summary, to provide a statistical description of the educational status of minorities in the state and the recent trends regarding minority participation in higher education.

Data Collection and Analysis. Initially, data collection and analysis efforts focused on data that were routinely gathered and maintained by the Indiana Commission for Higher Education from the public and independent institutions of higher education in the state. As is common in such efforts, the kinds of data used were often determined by what was available. The predominant time frame for the study, for example, was limited to the academic years 1978-79 through 1982-83, since these were the only years for which reliable racial data on students were available through the commission's Student Information System. Annual data, rather than fall enrollment data, were used simply because racial identifications were only available on the annualized records. One consequence of these limitations is that the study was criticized for its lack of timeliness (that is, reporting 1982-83 data in 1984) and for its short time frame from which to draw trends.

In the early stages of compiling the *Interim Report,* substantial effort was necessarily devoted to data correction and adjustments. The first summary of the data revealed to the advisory committee that the racial identifiers for one institution in one year were in error, so a new computer tape had to be created and incorporated into the data base. More troublesome was the number of students showing no racial identification, since institutional and other comparisons revealed different results, depending on the number of "unknowns." It was necessary, therefore, to estimate the number of minorities at each campus based on the percentage of those whose race was known.

One of the difficult issues early in the study was how to best report the data by race. It was relatively easy to maintain multiple data tables by the usual groupings: American Indian/Alaskan Native, Asian/Pacific Islander, black, Hispanic, and white. What became a problem was attempting to draw conclusions about minority participation, since the numbers and experiences of the groups differed markedly. The decision was made to report the data by race in the three categories of black, white, and other minority, while noting that the third classification is in fact a mixture of several disparate racial and nationality groups. This procedure allowed the study to focus on blacks, who made up 7.6 percent of the state's population, according to the 1980 census, while also giving some attention to the other minority groups making up a total of 2.1 percent of the population. The greatest benefit was in permitting the data summaries and conclusions to be simplified for presentation to the lay audience of policy makers to which the study was addressed.

Another of the data presentation and analysis decisions had to do with institutional types. Indiana's public system of higher education consists of two diverse multicampus university systems, Indiana University and Purdue University; the dual campus Indiana State University; the single campus Ball State University; a residential junior college, Vincennes University; and the thirteen campus Indiana Vocational Technical College. Despite the fact that within the public sector there are only six boards of trustees and presidents, substantial differences exist among the institutional campuses. In addition, there are thirty-three widely different independent colleges and universities enrolling a fourth of the 250,000+ students enrolled in higher education in the state.

As a result of the mix of public campuses and institutions, it is often more reasonable to compare individual campuses with similar characteristics, even if they are within different systems, than to compare the systems to each other. The decision was made to report the campus-by-campus data for the public and independent institutions to the institutional representatives on the advisory committee, but to report only institutional-level data publicly, with the independent institutions summarized as a single group. One other institutional classification was reported as well, that which distinguished campuses that are primarily residential from those that are primarily commuter in nature. This additional grouping yielded some interesting results concerning minority participation in higher education in the state, results that show that the type of campus may be a more useful level of analysis in some cases than the system of which it is part.

Results. Census data from 1970 and 1980 showed that the average educational attainments of blacks and most other minorities in the state were below those of whites, but that the gap has been reduced in recent years, particularly with regard to blacks. In 1980, for instance, 12.8 percent of whites over twenty-five years of age were college graduates as compared to 7.0 percent of blacks, but the proportion of black college graduates had increased 79.5 percent from 1970 to 1980. Likewise the percentage of high school graduates was lower for blacks than whites in 1980, 54.2 percent versus 67.3 percent, but the proportion had increased 52.5 percent from 1970 to 1980. In short, the census data concerning black educational achievements showed a group that remains educationally behind the majority, but that is catching up.

A related aspect revealed by the census data is the proportion of the black and other minority population that was below twenty-five years of age in 1980. While only 42 percent of whites were under twenty-five, 54 percent of blacks and 55 percent of other minorities were in the younger age group. In addition, the minority groups had increased as a proportion of the population from 1970 to 1980. The relative youth of minorities and their increasing proportion of the state's population demonstrates that the future of the Indiana colleges and universities will be connected inevitably to the enrollment and retention of blacks and other racial minorities.

Another source of racial data in education includes data

gathered by the state-level coordinating agency responsible for elementary and secondary educational matters, which in Indiana is now called the Department of Education. As seems to be common in many states, data concerning the number of high school graduates by year are unavailable, but it was possible to obtain trend data by race as to the number of students who are high school seniors and the number of school dropouts each year. The number of high school seniors peaked in 1978-79 in Indiana, but the number of high school dropouts of all races has been declining as well. As would be expected from a consideration of the census data, minorities constitute an increasing proportion of the high school seniors. A historically low participation rate in higher education, when matched with the mixed trends in high school attendance, suggests that increasing college participation rates might be a possibility in view of the smaller number of students in the traditional eighteen to twenty-two-year-old college age group. Substantial improvement in the participation rate, however, would have to include a higher participation rate among minorities.

One other source of precollege data that was tapped for the *Interim Report* was the College Board's Scholastic Aptitude Test, or SAT. A sobering statistic from that data source is that the number of black students taking the SAT declined more than 15 percent between 1978-79 and 1983-84, despite the increase in the proportion of blacks in the state's traditional college-age population. In other words, the number of blacks planning to go on to college appears to have declined, creating an even greater challenge to the state's system of higher education.

Enrollment data from the institutions of higher education in the state quickly revealed that the precollege data were a foreshadowing of college enrollments. While white enrollments increased 14.7 percent between 1978-79 and 1982-83 at public institutions, black enrollments increased only 5.5 percent. More disturbing, however, is the fact that black enrollments actually declined from 1979-80 to 1982-83. Declines and increases by institution tended to be proportionate to the number of blacks enrolled in prior years. Data comparability was a problem at the independent (private) colleges and universities, but they, too, seem to have experienced a similar pattern.

The types of campuses attended by black students shifted during the period, however. The residential campuses increased black enrollments slightly from 1978-79 to 1982-83, and the state's vocational-technical colleges enrolled 29 percent more students. But the commuter campuses of the state university system saw a decline of 5.5 percent. Likewise the greatest decline between 1980-81 and 1982-83 was at the commuter campuses, with the lowest being at the residential ones. Interestingly, similar data from the neighboring states of Illinois and Ohio for the same period showed similar results. The main differences are that Ohio's peak year for black enrollments came a year after Indiana's, and black enrollments in Illinois grew, but at a slower pace than those for whites. In both cases black enrollments shifted toward community colleges and technical programs and away from baccalaureate-granting institutions.

Several other demographic factors were examined in relation to race and enrollments; these are summarized below.

- By sex: An increasing proportion of both black and white students were female; blacks as a group have the highest proportion of female students of any racial group
- By full-time/part-time status: The proportion held relatively steady for all racial groups
- By degree program level: All groups saw declines in graduate enrollments and increases in lower-division enrollments, but only blacks declined at the baccalaureate level
- By legal residence: All groups showed increases in the proportion of students who were Indiana residents
- By age: The proportion of students twenty-five years of age and younger declined 4.4 percent for whites, but only 1.4 percent for blacks
- By academic discipline: All groups shifted toward more applied and technical disciplines and away from education, social sciences, and the humanities.

Final Report

Procedure. The data revealed disturbing trends, but there was no simple explanation for the decline in black enrollments. Since the causes and possible solutions were of paramount concern to all involved, the next logical step was to try to determine these. The procedure followed was to provide copies of the *Interim Report* to a number of knowledgeable individuals who, through their work or through their personal interests, would have valuable insights into the situation. The following groups were among those whose input was sought: the Indiana Black Caucus; the Indiana Coalition of Blacks in Higher Education; the advisory group on minority participation; college admissions and financial aid counselors; high school superintendents, counselors, and other high school staff; the state's Department of Education; and community organizations such as the Urban League. In general, cooperation was excellent, but none of the groups had a clear agenda as to what specific steps should be taken.

After a great deal of correspondence and a number of meetings with the groups and individuals just mentioned, several patterns of responses seemed to emerge, and these may be classified as follows: general comments, specific causes or reasons for the current situation, and possible ways of beginning to make changes.

Observations—General. It was interesting that most people who responded to the *Interim Report* said that the low rate of college participation was as much or more a precollegiate problem than one that the colleges and universities could significantly alter without help from the elementary and secondary schools. The critical age at which to influence students' decisions to go on to higher education was most often thought to be during junior high school, that is, seventh, eighth, and ninth grades. Many felt that high school was too late, since the high school course selection process and attitudes necessary to go on to higher education precede high school.

Another opinion heard frequently was that existing institutions and organizations ought to be better utilized, as opposed to creating new ones. The issue of black underrepresentation in higher education should not be addressed by creating new entities aimed at the problem, since the causes are within the existing structures and need to be dealt with there.

Observations—Perceived Causes. Among the perceived causes for low black participation in higher education in Indiana, as well as the recent decline in black enrollments, are the following:

1. *The Economy.* The downturn in the economy in the early 1980s, along with the resulting loss of jobs, had a disproportionately severe impact on minorities. Fewer blacks could afford to attend college.

2. *The Decline of Student Aid.* The per-student purchasing power of total state and federal student aid programs declined more than 31 percent in Indiana between 1979-80 and 1982-83.

3. *Improper Course Selection at the Elementary and Secondary School Levels.* The high school curriculum followed by black students in many cases makes the transition to college difficult, if not impossible; they often have not had the kinds of courses needed for successful college preparation.

4. *Inadequate Academic Preparation.* As a consequence of the causes cited in item 3 above, black students often have not acquired the basic academic skills necessary to successfully enroll in postsecondary study.

5. *High School Dropout Rates.* A higher proportion of blacks and other minorities drop out of high school, so that fewer are eligible to go on to college.

6. *Lack of Knowledge at an Early Age as to Possible Careers and the Kinds of Education Required in Those Career Fields.* This lack of academic and career information among younger black students too often allows them to make poor curriculum and other decisions at the secondary school level, thus limiting their options for postsecondary study.

7. *Lowered Enthusiasm for Educating Black Students.* In the 1960s and early 1970s many colleges and universities went through a period of actively recruiting minorities and providing them with special student services such as academic tutoring and special dormitories and cultural centers. The trend in recent years, caused in part by financial and legal constraints, has been to attempt more actively to integrate black students into the campus mainstream. There is a common belief that student services have been reduced in the process.

Many black high school graduates have seen this trend as a lack of commitment on the part of institutions of higher education to the unique needs of black students. Programs aimed at helping black students are no longer fashionable, they say, and are the first to be cut in times of restricted budgets. In addition, enrollments have continued to increase during the past five years without proportionate increases in black enrollment. All of this has occurred in the face of declining resources, so that black student participation is not seen as central to institutional survival.

8. *Admissions Requirements.* Although the data on admissions patterns are unavailable on a statewide basis, there is clearly a feeling among a substantial segment of the black community that institutions have raised their admissions requirements in recent years in response to fewer economic resources and attempts to raise academic standards. This trend is thought to be particularly true of programs in which student demand far exceeds the capability of institutions to admit all students interested in particular fields such as engineering, computer science, nursing, and business. Therefore, students who come to college with inadequate academic preparation

are among the first rejected from the kinds of high-demand programs that are most likely to lead to good jobs.

9. *The Complexities of Applying for Admission and Financial Aid at Institutions of Higher Education.* The financial aid process in particular requires substantial sophistication and perserverance to complete the detailed and complex forms that determine eligibility for aid and the amount of aid that may be expected. Application fees related to both admissions and financial aid also present barriers to those black students who come from homes with lower incomes. One result of this process is a high level of frustration, which can result in black high school graduates seeking alternatives to postsecondary education.

10. *Questions Concerning the Economic Value of Postsecondary Study.* The presence of unemployed and underemployed black college graduates in some communities has raised questions among secondary school students as to the employment benefits of higher education.

11. *Out-Migration.* Traditionally, a number of black students have chosen to attend predominantly black institutions in other states. In recent decades some have also left the state to enroll in predominantly white institutions. There is concern that black student out-migration may have accelerated during the 1978-79 to 1982-83 period. Although the data concerning black students attending colleges in other states are incomplete, there is at present no evidence of an acceleration of student out-migration.

Suggested Initiatives

A number of possible state initiatives grew out of the responses of the individuals asked to review the *Interim Report* concerning perceived causes for black underrepresentation and ways of addressing the causes. Following is a synopsis of the initiatives. (Note: Space requirements forced the editors to condense this section of the chapter. For further detail, please contact the author.)

Initiative #1: Provide adequate increases in state appropriation levels for student financial assistance to cover increases in fees and other costs as well as increases in the number of eligible recipients. In distributing grant aid, target funds to students having greatest need. Revise other criteria that limit the availability of funds to low-income students.

Initiative #2: Recommend that the Commission for Higher

Education, the college and university boards of trustees, and the State Board of Education take the initiative and recommend state-level partnership goals and recommend that each school corporation, in particular those with large concentrations of minority students, establish goals for related local participation rates in higher education. These goals should be highly publicized and firmly supported by the school boards and superintendents. As suggested by Governor Orr, the goal might be to reach the national average within five years. The goals should be monitored annually, with subsequent reports made to the school boards and to the State Board of Education. Reward structures might be established to provide incentives for successful efforts.

Initiative #3: Better counseling regarding postsecondary education and work is needed. Such efforts would use available technologies as well as existing human resources in the schools.

Initiative #4: Businesses and nonprofit organizations in metropolitan areas with large concentrations of minorities should agree to sponsor incoming minority college freshmen.

Initiative #5: The state should set aside a pool of funds to be used to pay the tuition costs of minorities with proven financial need. The advisory group on minority participation strongly recommended this initiative. The commission had addressed the need for improved funding of student aid and focusing student aid on the students with greatest financial need in its budget recommendations, however, so that commission staff did not support limiting a student aid program to a single group.

Initiative #6: Develop and disseminate widely a recommended high school course of study that states clearly which courses prepare students to enroll and succeed in an institution of higher education.

Initiative #7: The commission should discuss with the State Board of Education the possibility of suggesting that each school corporation in the state adopt a policy of requiring new high school students and their parents to sign a contractual arrangement with the school. Each contract would outline the type of curriculum recommended for successful admission into an institution of higher education or for immediately entering the job market (including military service) on graduation from high school. The curriculum would be among those recommended by state guidelines; several are currently available for both college and immediate employment after high school. The parents, in signing the contract, would acknowledge that they are aware of both state and nationally recommended curricula and their own child's high school curriculum. The student, in signing the contract, would acknowledge the existence of state standards, whether the high school courses that he or she chooses reflect that recognition or not. Institutions of higher education, as well as local employers and the military, would be encouraged to support and promote the use of such contracts. Some such contracts are currently in use in the state and are to be commended. (One school superintendent commented that implementing this initiative could lead to a bureaucratic nightmare.)

Initiative #8: Consideration should be given to continuing and expanding statewide efforts, such as the Higher Education Week sponsored by the Indiana Conference of Higher Education. Well-known civic, media, sports, and other personalities should speak on how pursuing postsecondary education helped change their lives and the lives of others. Institutions should provide special activities aimed at increasing public awareness of their programs and their contributions to the state.

Initiative #9: Institutions of higher education should be encouraged to expand the opportunities available in the special purpose activities aimed at secondary school students during the summer and the school year. One option would be to provide special scholarship opportunities to minority students of junior high school and early senior high school age. Included along with special purpose activities aimed at attracting students with special skills and interests would be academic and career counseling targeted to minority students with some potential for future college attendance. Additional state investments would be necessary to fund such programs.

Initiative #10: Policies and procedures need to be developed to gather and analyze data that are important to understanding minority underenrollment.

Observations and Prognostications

The current situation concerning black and other minority participation in postsecondary education in Indiana and elsewhere is obviously complex and fraught with difficulties. There seems to be a consensus that the noble experiments of the 1960s and 1970s, though well intentioned, were not very effective. There is also concern that blacks are no longer a major educational concern as a group; that their needs are no longer a fashionable topic of discussion in educational circles. Difficult financial conditions and increased enrollments at colleges and universities have led to reductions in programs aimed at helping minorities integrate into the mainstream of higher education. A lack of sophistication about the jobs and education necessary to succeed in a technological society is perceived as affecting all of those outside the great American middle class, most of whom are racial minorities. While there are no pat answers as to which specific actions are required or which ones would succeed, there is a strong feeling that something needs to be done soon to reverse the downward spiral.

It appears safe to say that minority underrepresentation will continue for the foreseeable future, until the pool of educated minority members increases, though improved economic conditions should compensate for some of the declines of recent years. Significant improvement will only come about, however, when minority youth become convinced at an early age that higher education does in fact lead to improved employment opportunities and a better quality of life. Commuter institutions in particular can have a significant impact due to their relative financial and geographical accessibility, which are critical to older as well as to younger college students who must often work at least part-time in order to afford higher education. Such institutions, however, must work at defining their own identities apart from the elitist traditions in which faculty members are trained, while still providing educational opportunities of the finest quality. It is truly a great challenge.

Improvement in the educational attainments of minorities will receive substantial help from the demographic realities of the future. It is inevitable that at some point, consensus will develop among the white population that increased educational attainment among minorities is needed in order for the country to remain competitive internationally in our changing technological economy. Unlike the situation in the 1960s, when the concern was for social equity, the next major efforts will be driven by enlightened self-interest among the majority population, for the proportion of blacks and other minorities in the workforce will continue to increase. Only a workforce in which most of the employees are skilled, well educated, or both will provide a secure economic future for the United States as a whole. Consequently, a common concern for economic survival, rather than a burning desire for social justice, will lead to significant educational improvement among minorities in the not-too-distant future.

References

Interim Report on Minority Student Participation. Indianapolis: Indiana Commission for Higher Education, 1984.
Profile of 1982-83 Recipients of Doctorates. Washington, D. C.: National Research Council, 1983.

John A. Muffo is director of special studies for the Indiana Commission for Higher Education and has served AIR in a number of capacities, including 1985 Forum chair. His research interests include the use of multivariate statistical techniques in sex and race discrimination cases.

The tools and skills necessary to defend against litigation are essential, but their potential goes well beyond litigation.

Concluding Remarks

William Rosenthal, Bernard Yancey

If there is a central theme to this volume, it is meant to be this: The tools and skills necessary to defend the institution against litigation are essential, but their potential goes well beyond litigation. Whether from the sense of social justice, which ought to motivate institutions of higher education, or from the sense of self-interest, our colleges and universities have the opportunity to study themselves, and having learned, to make important changes. The key to a successful response to social and equity issues is to develop a program for self-analysis that includes a well-designed self-study procedure combined with data bases that will permit the reconstruction or "capturing" of policy and practice at various times in the recent past. As Litwin points out, studies done and actions taken in the past do not guarantee that there is no longer a reason for careful self-study on a continuing basis.

Thus, this volume addresses itself to two of the possible responses to concerns about major social discrimination issues that affect faculty and staff: One response is to prepare to defend against some future litigation; the other is to create a system so equitable that no suits will be filed. As desirable as the latter is (and we argue for it), no amount of preparation or other ritual can guarantee that there will never be litigation; thus, just as it makes sense to buy liability insurance, it makes sense to create the data bases and analytic models for testing hypotheses of discrimination, unfairness, and inequity in order to ensure that the institution is well prepared should a staff member sue. Fortunately, to prepare well for one is to prepare for the other. Sound data kept in well designed data bases and accessible via sophisticated retrieval systems are essential for addressing the questions related to enlightened self-study as well as to litigation. In order to develop a set of questions to which the data analysis may be applied, data base designers need to review concerns ranging from those raised by Litwin in his discussion of institutional self-study to those raised by Yancey in his discussion of likely court case conditions. Not only will such a set of questions help to determine what data elements must be included, but the very activity of developing the questions will require that the institution review itself rigorously about its policies and practices. As is often true in large-scale planning exercises, the process itself may be valuable enough to warrant the activity. In addition, as institutional researchers well know, creating a data base often leads to questions from administrators that might not otherwise be asked.

No more than two or three years ago, the issue of who should create and maintain the data base would not have arisen. The administrative data-processing department would have been the only facility with access to the data and with the capability of building and maintaining a large data base. With the proliferation of data-manipulation systems such as the Statistical Analysis System (SAS), high powered microcomputers, and micro to mainframe linkages, many institutional research offices are fully capable of designing, building, and maintaining large longitudinal data bases. The merits of capability can only be discussed within the context of individual situation. However, the advantages of ease of access and ease of design change, as well as the advantage of quality control by the users of the data, must be considered against the disadvantage of the extra workload involved. Some data-processing departments will resist relinquishing control of data base functions, but that, too, is a situation that is changing rapidly.

Statistical methodology and the court is a topic about which much has been written but little seems to be known. The literature concerning what is wrong with or what errors are possible with regression models is becoming something of a cottage industry among statisticians in this field. Balanced against the arguments (many of them valid) of such statisticians are concerns about what the courts will allow or require, how to translate findings for a lay audience, and the possibility of using techniques that may provide more accurate results but that are even more difficult to explain to the court. Research offices that have not been through a court case are likely to take the view that certain data elements and methods of data collection and presentation are appropriate. The courts are likely to have a distinctly different view of what is acceptable or even required. Failure to develop a realistic view of what the courts are likely to accept may result in undesirable results ranging from doing a great deal of work a second time to severely harming the institution's case. Awareness and understanding of the statutes under which litigation can be brought and the basic models of proof that can be used to support the claims are essential, as is a basic understanding of the litigation process, including the various stages and requirements of each stage.

Although there can be no formula approach to deciding which procedures will apply or be useful in some future situation, consideration of the needs for various kinds of analysis will also help to determine what data elements must be kept and what formats and retrieval methods are most practical. These questions should also lead researchers to review their hardware and software resources, taking into account a set of critical considerations in the event of a sudden demand for sophisticated analyses. Although the algorithms used by statistical software do not appear to have become an issue in themselves, it seems only a matter of time until they become part of the courtroom debate, and researchers will need a strong argument for the logic of their software packages. One truly important criterion for statistical software is the clarity of its report formats.

Regrettably, many institutions have waited for the pressure of the court case or its threat to provide motivation to do the hard and expensive work of preparation for self-study. We believe that the benefits of preparedness are so self-evident that even the most hardened of financial vice-presidents should understand and second the desirability of being prepared. Furthermore, we believe that those efforts can and should consider society's needs as well as the self-interest of the institution. We submit Muffo's study of minority participation and involvement as one model of the kind of action research that has the potential for benefitting individuals, higher education, and society.

Like the studies discussed by Litwin, it draws on the impulse to improve rather than to accept conditions as they are or to accept stock answers to complex questions. Certainly, some part of our charge is to determine the success or failure of our institutions' activities and to use our research skills to study alternatives when we cannot confirm success. Muffo's point that the solutions of the past have often failed to produce the intended results is one that institutional researchers cannot take lightly. The redistribution of a small number of minority members among the institutions most able to bargain for their services does not address the real problems of minority representation in higher education, and this is a point the institutions themselves should not take lightly.

Suggestions for Further Reading

Chapter reference sections in this volume provide references for further study in this field. Beyond those sections, the literature in this area of concern is smaller than one might expect, but a few additional resources are worth mentioning.

Becker, G. S. *The Economics of Discrimination.* Chicago: University of Chicago Press, 1971.

A classic discussion of the concept of discrimination theory from the point of view of an economist.

Livernash, E. R. (Ed.). *Comparable Worth: Issues and Alternatives.* 2nd Edition. Washington, D. C.: Equal Employment Advisory Council, 1984.

A recent and reasonably comprehensive collection of papers with titles such as: "The Emerging Debate," "Job Evaluation and Pay Setting: Concepts and Practices," "The Market System," "Wage Setting Biases in the Measurement of Employment Discrimination," "The Legal Framework," and "An Analysis of the National Academy of Sciences' Comparable Study."

The Civil Rights Act of 1964. Washington, D. C.: Bureau of National Affairs, 1964.

While some of the material is rather dated, this volume still serves to provide a valuable perspective as to the original content and intent of the *Civil Rights Act of 1964.*

Lake, M. B. *Age Discrimination in Employment Act: A Compliance and Litigation Manual for Lawyers and Personnel Practitioners.* Washington, D. C.: Equal Employment Advisory Council, 1982.

This book provides an overview with respect to age discrimination, including the nature and content of the law and models of proof. Examples of statistical evidence that has been used are also presented.

The following government documents should also be considered:
Laws Administered by EEOC. Washington, D. C.: U.S. Government Printing Office, 1981.

Handy Reference Guide to the Fair Labor Standards Act. Washington, D. C.: U.S. Department of Labor, Employment Wage and Hour Division, WH Publication 1282, October 1978.

Journals containing pertinent articles would include the following:
Industrial and Labor Relations Review.
Monthly Labor Review.
Harvard Law Review.
The Journal of Business and Economic Statistics.
Columbia Law Review.
Virginia Law Review.
Labor Law Journal.
The Practical Lawyer.
Employee Relations Law Journal.

Additional information can be found in materials distributed through the *Clearinghouse for Civil Rights Research,* Center for National Policy Review, Catholic University School of Law, Washington, D.C., 20064.

William Rosenthal is professor of Institutional and Analytic Studies in the Office of Planning and Budgets at Michigan State University. He is currently involved in the development of large, mainframe-based analytic systems and in micro to mainframe applications.

Bernard Yancey, a research associate in the Office of the Dean of Students at the University of Texas at Austin, has been an expert witness in a variety of labor litigation cases and has conducted numerous workshops concerning the use of computers and statistics.

Index

A

Administrators: and discrimination studies, 12; and litigation defense team, 42
Advisory panels, for discrimination studies, 12-13
Age Discrimination in Employment Act of 1967 and amendments of 1978, 40, 63, 100
Albermarle Paper Co. v. *Moody*, 67, 80
Allard, C., 1, 19-34
Allen, W. R., 5, 8, 15
American Association of University Professors, 74
Anderson, R., 5, 15
Arpad, S., 10, 15
Association for Institutional Research, 19; Courts' Special Interest Group of, 1
Astin, A., 5, 14, 15
Astin, H., 14, 15

B

Baldus, D. C., 37, 38, 54, 63, 67, 71, 80
Ball State University, 86
Batson, S. W., 28, 33
Becker, G. S., 36, 63, 100
Bender, E., 15
Berg, H., 5, 15
Bevilacqua, N., 14, 16
Bickel, P. J., 68, 80
Bien, D. D., 50, 63
Birnbaum, M. H., 72, 78, 79, 80
Blanshan, S. A., 7, 15
BMD-P, 78
Board of Regents of the University of Nebraska v. *Dawes*, 70, 80
Bogart, K., 10, 15-16
Boulding, I. E., 36-37, 64
Braskamp, L. A., 74, 80
Brittingham, B. E., 67, 69, 71, 81
Brown, G., 14, 16
Brown, M. H., 22, 28, 34
Burk, B., 15

C

Castaneda v. *Partida*, 50, 64
Chicago, University of, paired-comparison method at, 68
Chizmar, J. F., Jr., 67, 81
Civil Rights Acts of 1866 and 1971, 38-39
Civil Rights Act of 1964, 100; Title VI of, 39; Title VII of, 38-39, 50-51, 66, 67
Clark, D. L., 29, 34
Class certification: defendant's strategies during, 51-53; defining class for, 50-51; and discretionary power, 51; as litigation stage, 49-53; and statistical evidence, 51-53; strategies in, 51
Cohen, J., 70, 71, 80
Cohen, P., 70, 71, 80
Cole, J. W. L., 37, 38, 54, 63, 67, 71, 80
College Board, 88
Comparison studies, for discrimination studies, 11-12
Cones, J. H., III, 5, 8, 16
Confidence limits, hyperbolic, and salary adjustment, 78-79
Courts: and assessment of salary equity, 29; litigation in, 35-64; and monitoring system, 29-33; specifications by, 29; and statistical issues, 65-82
Crawford, S., 3n, 4, 16
Crocker, P., 7-8, 16

D

Daniel, C., 75, 80
Data base: and baselines, 30-31; on campus personnel, 25-26; conclusions on, 97-100; longitudinal, 26-28; problems of, 20; for salary equity research, 19-34; variables included in, 27-28
Daughtry, D., 15

103

Decision support group, and litigation defense team, 43-44
Department of Education (Indiana), 88, 90
Department of Public Instruction (Indiana), 85
DiNunzio, J., 17
Discovery: defendant's objectives in, 47-49; plaintiff's objectives in, 47, 57-63; pre-trial preparation during, 49; stage of, 46-49
Discrimination: conclusions on, 97-100; journals on, 101; litigation alleging, 35-64; mechanisms of, 36-37; and minority participation, 83-96; readings on, 100-101; and salary equity research, 19-34; and statistical issues, 65-82; statutes covering, 38-41; studies of, 3-17
Discrimination studies: and administrators, 12; analysis of, 3-17; background on, 3-6; barriers to, 4-5; beginning, 12-14; conclusions on, 14-15; context for, 13-14; defining terms for, 7-9, 13; design steps for, 6-12; and institutional statistics, 6-7; methods selection for, 10-12, 13; purpose of, 9-10, 13; reasons for, 5-6; responses to, 14
Disparate impact, as model of proof, 37-38
Disparate treatment, as model of proof, 37
Draper, N. 78, 80
Duran, R., 14, 16
Dziech, B. W., 5, 6, 8, 15, 16

E

Engelmayer, P., 5, 16
Equal Employment Opportunity Commission, 39, 41, 45, 58, 101
Equal Pay Act of 1963, 40, 64
Expert, and litigation defense team, 44-45, 53
Exum, W., 9, 15, 16

F

Facial discrimination, as model of proof, 37
Fair Labor Standards Act of 1938, 40, 101

Faro v. *New York University*, 66, 69, 80
Farrell, J., 5, 16
Ferber, M. A., 5, 15, 74, 80
Fincher, C., 14, 16
Finkelstein, M. O., 67, 74, 80
Fisher, F., 67, 71, 79, 80
Flagle, J., 15-16
Ford Foundation, 14
Forrest, L., 5, 13, 16
Franklin, P., 14, 16

G

Gartland, D., 14, 16
General Telephone Co. of the Southwest v. *Falcon*, 51, 64
Gosman, E., 12, 16
Gray, M. W., 67, 80
Greenfield, E., 69, 71, 80
Griggs v. *Duke Power Co.*, 67, 80

H

Hall, R., 8, 11, 16
Hammel, E. A., 80
Harvard University, administrative support at, 12
Hazelwood School District v. *United States*, 50, 64, 66, 80
Hengstler, D. D., 2, 65-82
Hengstler, G. W., 80
Hinkle, D. E., 78, 80
Hitt, M., 12, 16
Hoffmann, E. P., 74, 80

I

Illinois, minority participation in, 89
Indiana, minority participation in, 83-89
Indiana Coalition of Blacks in Higher Education, 83-84, 89
Indiana Commission for Higher Education, 83, 84, 85, 92-93
Indiana Conference of Higher Education, 94
Indiana State University, 86
Indiana University, 86
Indiana Vocational Technical College, 86
Institutional research, litigation roles for, 35-64. *See also* Data base; Salary equity research; Statistics

International Brotherhood of Teamsters v. United States, 50, 64, 66, 80
Interviews, for discrimination studies, 11

J

Jackson, J., 84
Janha, D., 16
Jenkins, M., 9, 11, 16
Johnson, G. E., 74, 80
Jones v. Alfred H. Mayer Co., 39, 64
Jung, S., 15-16

K

Katz, D. A., 74, 81
Katz, J., 8, 16
Keats, B., 16
Kennedy, J. J., 78, 81
Kent, L, 14, 15
Kerlinger, F. N., 70, 81
Keys v. Lenoir Rhyne College, 68, 81
Koch, J. V., 67, 81
Kordick, B., 74, 80

L

Lake, M. B., 100
Langston, I. W., III, 1, 19-34, 80
Legal staff, and litigation defense team, 42-43
Linn, R. L. P., 75, 81
Litigation: analysis of, 35-64; background on, 35-36; class certification stage of, 49-53; discovery stage of, 46-49; and experts, 44-45, 53; models of proof for, 36-38; stages of and strategies for, 46-57; statutes appropriate for, 38-41; strengths and weaknesses in positions in, 41-42; summary on, 57; team to defend against, 42-46; timing in, 45-46; trial stage of, 53-57
Litwin, J. L., 1, 2, 3-17, 97, 98, 99
Livernash, E. R., 100
Log-linear models, and multiple regression statistics, 76-78
Logit analysis, and multiple regression statistics, 76, 77-78

M

McCullagh, P., 75, 81
McDonnell Douglas Corp. v. Green, 66, 67, 81

McLaughlin, G. W., 2, 65-82
McPherson, M., 15, 16
Mahan, B. T., 81
Maihoff, N., 5, 13, 16
Maryland at College Park, University of, salary equity review at, 22-23, 25-26
Maynard, B. J., 67, 81
Mecklenburg v. Montana Board of Regents of Higher Education, 69, 74, 81
Menges, R., 9, 15, 16
Metha, A., 7, 10, 16
Minority participation: analysis of, 83-96; background on, 83-84; context for, 84-85; data collection and analysis on, 85-87; final report on, 89-92; findings on, 87-89; future of, 94-95; interim report on, 84-89; observations on, 90; perceived causes of, 90-92; reporting procedure on, 89-90; suggested initiatives for, 92-94
Monitoring systems: baselines for, 30-31; court-ordered, 29-33; internally motivated, 19-28; and litigation, 36, 42, 46, 49, 57; modifying, 32-33; using, 31-32
Muffo, J. A., 2, 71, 80, 81, 83-96, 99-100
Multicollinearity, and predictors, 72
Multiple regression statistics: assumptions of, 75-76; limitations of, 71-79; and predictors, 71-74; and reverse regression, 79; in salary equity research, 70-71; and samples, 74-75

N

National Research Council, 84
Nelder, J. A., 75, 81
Networking, for discrimination studies, 13
Nevill, D. D., 67, 69, 81
Nigg, J., 7, 10, 16
Noonan, J. F., 16

O

Ochsner, N. L., 28, 34
O'Connel, J. W., 80
Ohio, minority participation in, 89
Orr, R. D., 93
Otero v. Mesa County Valley School District, 66, 81

P

Paired-comparison method, for salary equity research, 68-69
Panos, R., 7, 16
Patton, M. Q., 11, 17
Payne, C., 76, 78, 81
Pedhazur, E. J., 70, 81
Peterson, M., 12, 17
Pezzullo, T. R., 67, 69, 71, 81
Pomrenke, V., 14, 17
Prather, J. E., 69, 81
Presseisen v. *Swarthmore College*, 69, 74, 81
Project on the Status and Education of Women, 5, 12, 14, 17
Public Meetings, for discrimination studies, 11
Purdue University, 86
Purdum, S., 16

Q

Qualitative methods, for discrimination studies, 11
Questionnaires, for discrimination studies, 10

R

Racism: institutional, concept of, 9; and minority participation, 83-96; studying, 3-17. *See also* Discrimination
Reagan, B. B., 67, 81
Regression analysis, for salary equity studies, 69-70
Rehabilitation Act of 1973, 40-41, 64
Rosenthal, W. H., 1-2, 28, 34, 67, 68, 71, 81, 97-101
Rosovsky, H., 12

S

Salaries: adjustment of, and multiple regression statistics, 78-79; processes affecting levels of, 21-22
Salary equity research: analysis of, 19-34; background on, 19-21; constraints on acting on, 24-25; and court-ordered monitoring, 28-33; focus of, 21-23; internally motivated monitoring of, 19-28; interpretation of findings from, 23-24; longitudinal data base for, 26-28; monitoring system for, 29-33; personnel data base for, 25-26; statistical issues in, 65-82; variables in data base for, 27-28
Santangelo, L., 50, 63
Schmidtlein, F. A., 1, 19-34
Scholastic Aptitude Test (SAT), 88
Scott, E. L., 67, 73, 74, 80, 81
Sexism: and salary equity research, 19-34; and statistical issues, 65-82; studies of, 3-17. *See also* Discrimination
Sexual harassment, defining, 7
Simpson, W. A., 28, 34, 67, 68, 81
Single-group studies, for discrimination studies, 11-12
Smith, D., 5, 17
Smith, G., 69, 81
Smith, H., 78, 80
Spaulding, C., 17
Sperber, W. E., 81
SPSSX, 78
Stafford, F. P., 74, 80
Stastny v. *Southern Bell Telephone & Telegraph Co.*, 73, 81
State Board of Education (Indiana), 93
Statistical Analysis System (SAS), 26, 76, 78, 98
Statistics: analysis of issues in, 65-82; conclusion on, 79; court reactions to, 65-66; and descriptive method, 67-68; multiple regression, 70-79; with paired-comparison method, 68-69; with regression analysis approach, 69-70; in salary equity studies, 67-70
Stone, W., 3n
Strickler, G. M., Jr., 38-39, 40, 64
Student Perception Questionnaire, 11
Students: minority, participation by, 83-96; ratings by, for discrimination studies, 11
Sweeney v. *Board of Trustees of Keene State College*, 66, 81

T

Terrass, S., 3n, 14, 17
Test of association, and multiple regression statistics, 76-77
Thomas, G. E., 5, 14, 17
Thurow, L. C., 36, 64

Trial: audience for, 55-56; credibility during, 54-55; depositions and affidavits for, 56-57; as litigation stage, 53-57; strategies during, 54; testifying at, 54-57
Tribe, L. H., 37, 64
Trout v. *Hidalgo*, 70, 75, 82

U

U.S. Bureau of National Affairs, 39, 64
U.S. Bureau of the Census, 85
U.S. Department of Labor, 41
Urban League, 90

V

Verba, S., 14, 17
Vincennes University, 86

W

Walker, N., 15
Weiner, L., 5, 6, 8, 15, 16
Wilkins v. *University of Houston*, 70, 71, 73, 82
Wilson, K., 15
Wood, F. S., 75, 80

Y

Yancey, B., 1-2, 28, 34, 35-64, 97-101

Z

Zirkes, M. B., 81